TEACHING TV ADVERTISING

Wendy Helsby

Contents

Aims and Rationale

'More than just the ticket' (British Airways travel shop)

The aim of this book is to give an insight and understanding into the advertising industry and specifically that of television advertising. The areas covered include a historical perspective, the advertising industry and its guidelines, textual analysis, and ways to study audiences and the messages they read. There are discussion points in each section that can be used to springboard or stimulate thoughts around the issues being raised and there are activities at the end of each section. These can be adapted for individual or class use and are aimed at developing the points made in that section. In addition there are a resource list and a bibliography/reference to help both teachers and students in further research. The resource list includes websites on some of the issues and campaigns cited, for example the Benetton campaign, as well as resources currently available. There are several worked examples, an imaginary case study and a possible classroom schedule with lesson plans in the appendix.

(N.B. In this book the word *advertisement* is sometimes shortened to *advert* and occasionally *ad*.)

Introduction

Television advertising is about communication. At its most basic it provides information, and arouses our interest in a service or a commodity for sale. It uses both visual and sound languages. But television is only one of the media through which advertising works: magazines, newspapers, radio, cinema and of course the newer forms of mobile phones and the Internet, as well as publicity billboards, buses, trains and taxis, tennis shirts and well placed bottles at Wimbledon all provide opportunity for advertising. This is huge business. It is a business with its own history and archives. It has its own award ceremonies. It has regulators in each of the media. It has agencies whose role is to provide a total service for companies and organisations wishing to advertise. These agencies employ talented and creative people to make adverts and specialist researchers to look at the target markets.

Advertisements can influence us directly and indirectly. You may as an individual be persuaded to purchase a particular **brand**. You might also as a member of the public be aware of **icons** being created. What consumer brand do you think of when you see Gary Lineker. What shop do you think of that is 'never knowingly under sold'?

Gary Lineker struggles with temptation in a Walkers ad

Advertising can become a news story and be the subject of documentaries. Benetton became infamous for their advertising campaign controversy and were the subject of at least two documentaries.

Advertisements are part of the society in which, and for which, they are created. There are many resources looking at the history of advertising and just a flick through old advertisements will reveal attitudes about class, gender, nationalities and race amongst the matrix of attitudes that formed a society's **ideological** position in the past. In a sense therefore advertisements become the unwitting testimony of the present.

How will the future see our present? Having completed your work on advertising you might like to come back to this question and see whether you could formulate an answer from your study of television advertisements.

Theory

There are many ways to approach advertising as an area of Media Studies. One area is to study the texts as objects to be read as creative pieces. However it is also possible to see advertisements as cultural constructions reflecting a pluralist society. Others would see them as part of a manipulation of society to aid consumption and contribute to capital. Each approach comes from a different theoretical perspective, such as; a structuralist, culturalist, Marxist, feminist, or **postmodernist**, each having a different focus on the role of advertising in society. These are not mutually exclusive theories, and each reveals something different about the complex world of advertising.

Introduction and Theory

Early years

The early study of advertising in the first half of the twentieth century as a means of communication was wrapped up with the critique of society and the capitalist system. These views were based upon Marcuse and the Frankfurt School of thought that took an anti-capitalist view. As a result much critical research addressed the social and cultural effects of advertising from a perspective that saw the audience as basically passively reading a distorted message with major ideological impact.

Later research such as Goffman (1972) on gender and Williamson (1978) on ideology examined the content and structure of advertising for the ideological messages hidden in the text. Using the deconstruction techniques of **semiotics** (Saussure, 1927) and content analysis they studied the detail of the text at the micro level. In contrast to this micro emphasis other works took a macro look at the advertising industry as part of a larger social and political structure. Works such as Vince Packard's *The Hidden Persuaders* (1957), an early criterion of advertising effects, criticised the techniques used to persuade. This critique used the **hypodermic** or **bullet model** of media effects. The model is one that suggests that there is an immediate effect on behaviour. It suggests a passive consumer and a short-term effect. It has been criticised for being too simplistic in its approach. Others have changed the focus on to the inequalities in the relationship between advert and consumer by focusing on the power, both economic and cultural, in the hands of a few corporations. Noam Chomsky has argued this point particularly in relation to the news agenda in the United States. It is this area that has contributed to the debate on globalisation and cultural imperialism. Multinationals such as McDonalds and Coca-Cola have been criticised for using their immense economic power to impose their products upon local cultures.

Advertising and meanings

'Live the difference' Renault

Why do we have advertising? What is its function? Advertising gives us information; it plays a role in social communication as in campaign advertisements such as drink driving or health campaigns. It provides the oil to lubricate the consumer capitalist society in which we work and live by promoting products and services we may wish to use. In so doing advertising uses a complex set of **codes** and **symbolism**. But some would argue that it also has a social function in that it mediates social roles through its **discourse**.

One way in which it communicates is to differentiate in the way it speaks to its audience. At one level we can see that women are addressed differently than men. For women, romance and family are often used; and for men machismo and the friendship group are the strategies employed. These approaches may have shifted slightly through time but their core psychology still holds true. Where adverts have changed is in the style of address. The use of visuals has become dominant so that visual literacy is an essential skill for reading adverts. This literacy, like other literacies, has to be learnt. An advertising image is not 'just a picture'; it has been carefully constructed with every element contributing to the overall message and the thousand words it contains.

NOTES:

Adverts have become more complex and sophisticated in how they deliver their message. A classic example of this would be the Silk Cut cigarette adverts. Here a purple strip of silk material was cut by a sharp implement such as a pair of scissors. There was no need for any further information. The image conveyed the brand, Silk Cut and the colour matched the product on the shelf. Another example was a drink, American Dry. A baseball player stood next to a white horse. The message was seen through the iconicity, the American game and the brand image.

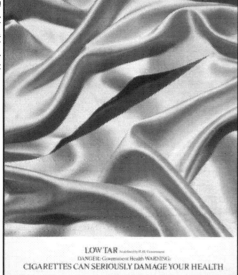

Silk Cut – the ad says it all

But a brand message is also aligned to other meanings. In essence the meanings associated with the products are often more important than the functions to which the products are put (Leiss, et al., 1986). In a consumer society it is argued that our gratification is through consumption and the consumer's definition of status in society is defined through this consumption. This is often called the **uses and gratification** theory. Advertisers therefore want to align the products they are selling to lines of appeal such as status, life styles, values and pleasures that would gratify the needs aroused in the consumer. Thus advertising tells consumers which product they 'need' to achieve their perceived goals in terms of coolness, success, popularity, status and so on. Products become social communicators that function in our interpersonal world. Just as we communicate by looks, hand movements and so on, so we communicate by our consumption, whether it be a car or a trainer. This creates a **fetishistic** consciousness, where the products and services have symbolic values associated with the socially desirable attributes. So the

brand or **logo** is as important as the product, whether it be a Swatch or a Rolex watch it conveys a message beyond an object that tells the time accurately. Thus advertising has a social function.

In culture, boundaries for behaviour or attitudes are formed: within the boundary will have positive connotations and beyond negative social connotations. These are moving boundaries or paradigms as social, cultural, economic and other factors help to change attitudes in society. Advertisers must respond and if they get it wrong then the product will not be used by the consumer and it will disappear or become re-branded. It has also been argued that consumers have a sense of codes of consumption that convey a hierarchy of values and prestige, as with the example of the watches. If this is so then the needs are socially constructed and their exchange for goods has a value. Baudrillard pointed to the idea of exchange and sign value as part of the 'game' of consumption to which advertisers must respond.

Advertising confirms or marks certain behaviour and beliefs (ideologies) as either dominant or deviant. These include the issue of **representation** of gender, race and other role models that are sanctioned by the way that images are viewed (or marked by their absence) in adverts. It is for this reason that researchers such as Goffman and Williamson have been critical of advertising imagery: 'The result is a culture where image plays a more important role than linguistic discourse, for while verbal imagery is discursive, visual imagery is non-discursive, emotional, associative, iconic, and fictive' (Harms and Kellner, www.uta.edu/english).

An illustration of this point was the image of Tony Blair during a General Election campaign with the superimposed 'horror eyes'. This image arguably had more political impact for the Conservative party than all their election pamphleteering (although they still lost the election heavily). Political campaigning is a form of advertising. Political parties have employed advertising agencies to develop their messages. The use of advertising techniques in public rather than commercial discourse has led to much debate about the ethical implications. If politicians use image rather than rational appeal then is democracy under threat?

Introduction and Theory

To return to consumer advertising: in Marxist ideology the creation of an image through aesthetics and advertising creates markets, the 'superstructure', and supports the capitalist economy, the 'base'. The promise of happiness is through consumption. This is the 'culture industry' as described by Adorno. It distracts people from the important issues and exploits and manipulates rather than arouses involvement and action. The capitalist system forces business to maximise profits at the cost of individual freedom of choice. The creation of needs must continue. This explains why 'new', 'better', 'improved' commodities appear in advertisements. The consumer has to be persuaded to consume the same product again and again in multifarious forms that change chameleon-like but are in essence the same product; or build in obsolescence, or strive for the unattainable image, such as of youth as the consumer ages...'**because you're worth it**'. The use of image to sell develops a belief about the self that is constructed by the advertising industry and therefore indirectly by 'big business'.

Advertising's position in the mass media facilitates the control of culture by the large organisations that use it. In other words the means of production and culture are both relevant in looking at advertising. It is both an economic force as well as having cultural and ideological impact. This means that advertising is seen to have short-term effects in persuading people to buy but also long-term effects in selling ideas and role models.

For the study of the latter the work of Judith Williamson has been seminal. She studied adverts for both their semiotic construction and their ideological meanings. This followed the work begun by Roland Barthes (1972) where he argued for a level of analysis that used the **denotative** and **connotative** readings to reveal the deeper 'mythic' meaning. Judith Williamson's analyses of the construction of gender and class in adverts provided a commentary on social issues, as for example the use of nature as an attribute for manufactured goods: '"The Natural" is the meaning given by culture to nature; ...Thus society works on nature in two ways: with technology, to create manufactured goods, and with ideology, to create symbols of "the natural" which are then juxtaposed with the manufactured goods so that meaning may be exchanged between the two' (1978, p. 123). She goes on to explain and illustrate how the natural is used to connote perfection, danger, obviousness, naughtiness and other qualities. These are seen as desirable when nature is connected with them. Nature is therefore given a moral value.

Williamson also looked at the way 'magic' and our belief in the magical transformation is used and in the use of narrative and history. Any study of an advertising campaign either for a single brand or for a range of brands can reveal similar links between ideas and products such as around individuality, sexuality, patriotism and heritage. They are a means of conveying and revealing social trends. Consumers seem willing to spend more on a product that is apparently socially desirable rather than cheap, particularly for image products such as personal goods. The emotional appeal overcomes economic reason.

One factor that affects the power of advertising is that of ownership. In recent years there has been a move for communication companies to merge to create large **conglomerates**. This creates a **synergy** through which the power of the new company can expand in all its forms

NOTES:

of communication. One classic example is that of the AOL Time Warner conglomerate. Here the control, by one group, of ideas and messages could be seen to be significant not only for America but also globally. The issue is one that can be addressed in looking at global brands such as fast food and soft drinks. Companies such as Nescafé, McDonalds and Coca-Cola have global interests. The control of the message may lead to more limited messages and less diversity of culture. It could also lead to less diversity in products as larger companies use their advertising power to squeeze out any local rivals.

Advertising is the dominant financial support for most forms of popular communication, such as radio, television, magazines and newspapers. It is not unlikely therefore that advertisers could influence content. There has recently been the debate in Britain about the 'dumbing down' of television programming. Advertisers are interested in the mass market and maximising audience numbers. The appeal to this mass audience is often through sensationalism, sex, violence and thrills. There is, it is therefore claimed, a trend to spice up programmes with large audiences, such as soap operas, or to develop more sensational programmes such as reality TV with the *Big Brother* style phenomenon, to attract the audience.

In all media products the adverts 'interrupt' the content. But without advertising how would these companies survive? Does the consumer benefit because we have a relatively cheap mass media? It would certainly be a very expensive newspaper or magazine that did not have any advertising. One only has to see this by costing out the production of a student magazine. Even where there are no overhead costs a relatively simple product becomes the same price as a commercial magazine. So does advertising subsidise our media consumption? The answer may be 'no', as *someone* has to pay. In all likelihood, the cost will eventually be passed on to the consumer through the price of the product.

immediate effect is to try to get us to buy a product, but it also has long-term effects through repetition of messages such as ideologies. As a text it reflects historical changes within society. Although apparently a superficial and ephemeral activity, the history of advertising could be seen as the history of modern consumer society. This is why the study of television advertising is an important part of the study of the media.

So, how *will* the future see our present through television advertising?

'It's a different whiteness' – Oxydol

Conclusion

Advertising has the power to appeal to needs and desires of consumers through the use of images and verbal languages. Its

The Advertising Industry

Discuss

Memory Lane

What advertising campaigns have you enjoyed; or remember; or think were clever; or disliked completely?

'Yaris – You could love it too much'

Advertising is part of our world. You are probably wearing something at the moment which sports a **logo**. It appears around us in our physical environment and in our communication with the world. With the increasing use of the media and its developing interactivity advertising is shaping our personal space in subtle and sophisticated ways.

1.1 Does advertising work?

In 2004 advertisers were paying £1m and more for a 30 second advertising slot in the last episode of the C4 sitcom *Friends* (Cozens, *The Guardian*, 20 January 2004), whilst the 2004 Super Bowl finale to the American Football season could charge £1.2m for a 30 second slot. In 2000 the Super Bowl generated £92m in advertising revenue. If advertising doesn't work, as is sometimes asserted, someone is paying a whole lot of money for very little return. Why pay this amount of money? Look at the audience numbers. In 2003 there were 90 million viewers of the Super Bowl final in the USA and internationally. It beat the Rugby World Cup for viewing figures in spite of its parochial USA nature ('Advertisers take punt on Super Bowl', Cozens, *The Guardian* 15 January 2004).

Who signs up for these slots? They are multi-national companies such as Pepsi and Proctor and Gamble (washing powder) as well as forthcoming Hollywood films. The advertisements are also sometimes made by film directors. Ridley Scott (*Alien*, 1979) who made the Hovis adverts for British television was used by Apple in 1984 to make its award winning commercial. Another successful British director who worked on commercials is Alan Parker who made the Heineken Galley Slave advert; and Anthony Minghella has signed up for the new Guinness campaign (*The Daily Telegraph*, 27 August 2004).

How do adverts work? People will often claim that they are not influenced by adverts. The evidence refutes this and shows that good advertising *does* work. **Agencies** such as Saatchi & Saatchi have built huge businesses on the success of their campaigns. Advertisers appeal through the dreams and aspirations of the consumer. Which mother would not want a happy baby? And if a particular brand of nappies does it then surely that is *the* brand to buy. Or which pet owner doesn't want a lively, healthy animal; or housewife washing that is cleaner and whiter; or a young person a holiday full of eastern promise…it is the role of advertising to create these needs in us. There is an acronym for the way advertisements work. It is DRIP:

D – differentiates a company's products;

R – reassures and reminds consumers of the benefits of the products or services;

I – informs people about an advertiser's products, services or cause;

P – persuades people that they should believe what they see in the ad and to take action in light of it. (**ASA** web site)

1.2 History of advertising

'It's tingling fresh. It's fresh as ice. It's Gibbs SR' – the first UK television ad

Advertising your goods and services has been around for centuries, but mass advertising has really only developed since newspapers became the first form of mass communication in the eighteenth century. Most of these were simple adverts telling of a particular product or sale. Any claims were never questioned. The Pears soap adverts was the first really significant campaign. By the late nineteenth century advertising agencies had been established to deal with creating campaigns. In Britain

MRS GEORGINA WELDON

WRITES:
"24 MAY 1887"

'I am "50" to-day"

"but, thanks to "Pears Soap"

"My COMPLEXION is only 17."

© The Advertising Archive

Pears Soap – first ad campaign

adverts were still limited to print and in the cinema. In other parts of the world advertising used radio and later television to deliver its message. In America the use of a series of adverts within one show was developed and this became known as the *commercial break*. In the United Kingdom television advertising was admitted in 1955 when ITV was launched. The regulation of adverts was also introduced at the same time through the TV regulators, at first the ITA (the Independent Television Authority), followed by the IBA and then the ITC until 2003 with the arrival of Ofcom.

1.3 The advertising agency

It is the advertising agencies who create adverts. They develop a campaign having been given a brief by the company or organisation, such as a charity, paying for the advert, such as Abbot Mead Vickers BBDO agency who developed the Guinness 'surfers' ad with the horses.

These are companies whose talent is communication. There are many famous names in this area such as Saatchi & Saatchi, but there are also many smaller

companies who provide marketing campaigns. The advertising agency's job is to develop the campaign and nurture it to completion.

A TV advertisement's journey from concept to screen could look something like this.

- The company rings up an advertising agency such as Saatchi and Saatchi or one of the many smaller ones.

- The client and the agency meet and decide a strategy and budget. The brief is decided.

- The job is given to an account manager who follows the project through all its stages and ensures it keeps to budget.

- The creative director and the account planners consider a strategy and develop the campaign.

- Market research tells them about the target market and suggests images and lines of appeal.

- The creative team now design the advertisement.

- The campaign is approved by the client – or not – and if not, it's back to the drawing board!

- The storyboard is vetted by the Broadcasting Advertising Clearance Centre.

- The advertisement is made. If it's a big campaign the agency may use well known directors from the film industry as well as television.

- The media planner will decide how best to reach the target market and whether to test various options.

- Under the direction of the media planner, the media buyers will buy space on television. They will try to optimise the effect of the advertisement by buying the best time slot for the budget available.

- The advertisement is on television.

- The market research evaluates its effectiveness by using focus groups and by quantitative research such as ratings. The company sees if sales have gone up in the region where the campaign was running. (Remember regional television means that on ITV1 advertisements may not be seen simultaneously all over the country.)

This sounds a foolproof system for success but as the commercial world gets more cluttered, especially with the fragmentation of audiences as a result of digitalisation, and the audiences metaphorically switch off, advertising has had to develop new strategies:

'There has been a massive proliferation and fragmentation of all types of media, but consumers do not consume more media; they are more selective in their diet and consume it less thoroughly. The challenge for advertisers is to create differentiation and impact…' (Tom Manwaring, director of strategy and planning at media buying agency Initiative Media, quoted in 'Ads on eggs? They must be going bananas', Rosenbaum, *The Independent*, 13 December 1994).

1.4 Advertising – what is its role?

There are two key tasks for advertising:

- the market/consumer has to identified;

- the message has to be created that suggests to the consumer something about themselves and about their personal image (this is the **line of appeal**).

In broadcast adverts this message is more important that any information about the product. For example, a product such as a mobile phone would identify several users/consumers such as the teenager, businessman, vulnerable or disabled person. The line of appeal would have to be very different for each of these groups. The teenager would be interested in the gizmos; its cheapness to run; its fashion

statement; its coolness and so on. The businessman would want to know its effectiveness in storing information; its reliability; maybe its added functions such as a calculator. The vulnerable person may wish to know its ease of use; how heavy to carry or hold. Each of these groups would need a different advertising campaign.

The lines of appeal that were evident in earlier advertising were ones such as snob appeal, fear and one-up-man-ship. In the decades after World War II, class status was deeply ingrained in society. The sixties, with its loosening of censorship codes, speeded up a process that had already started to move our interest from class appeal to sex appeal and consumerism. Advertisers have continued to use this very successful association in many products from chocolate flakes to cars. Sex does sell.

The MGB GT V8 version ad, from 1973

Advertisers have relied upon marketing research to identify lines of appeal and to help create the needs in the audience. Research is difficult and the audience can be fickle. A direct question can lead to an evasive answer or a respondant wanting to appear sophisticated and so ratchets up their actual choice of product. Sophisticated techniques have therefore been developed through **focus groups** and **psychological techniques**. For example, the Guinness advertisements that focused on its Celtic image with the harvesting of wheat by scythe were inspired by research amongst consumers who produced 'psycho drawings' or **psychographics** that showed that the Celtic associations of the drink strongly appealed. The Guinness campaign for the nineties, in contrast, focused upon the individuality that people were expressing at the time and delivered a serious of surreal adverts with actor Rutger Hauer personifying the glass of Guinness with his black clothes and pale head.

© The Advertising Archive

Cheers! Rutger Hauer raises a glass to one of the most memorable TV ad campaigns

This illustrates how advertisers have to be very aware of current trends and movements in society. This appeal to individuality would not have worked in earlier decades. So advertisers need to reflect society as well as hoping to establish new needs and trends in the market. Association with wishes, desires, social trends are important in developing campaigns that may go across several media; print, radio, cinema as well as television. Repetition of the message through associations as well as through different media is important for the recognition of the brand. Much time and effort is therefore expended in trying to find these trends. Agencies will 'employ' teenage consultants to tell them what's 'in' for street fashion; what is the latest language; is 'cool' still 'cool'? In *A Hard Day's Night* (1964) George Harrison finds himself inside a television production office where style programmes for the new teenage consumer market are being produced. Harrison 'rubbishes' the new fashions and faces it is trying to promote and is unceremoniously chucked out of the office.

So advertisements have relatively little information about the product, but quite a lot about the potential purchaser

1.5 Television – a pott-ad history

The first UK television advertisement was shown on Independent Television, when it began broadcasting in 1955, for Gibbs SR toothpaste. International firms, especially based in America, had already been using television advertising as the majority of stations were commercial. **Product placement** and **sponsorship** became just part of the scenery of watching television in the USA. For example, the news presenter might interrupt the news to light up his 'favourite' cigarette brand. But in the United Kingdom advertising on television had been impossible as the BBC was the only broadcaster and its Public Service Broadcaster (PSB) remit and its funding through the licence fee meant that it did not carry advertisements or use sponsorship.

ITV on the other hand was funded by its advertising and therefore had to sell as much advertising space as it was allowed (there was a limit imposed) between programmes and in programme breaks. As the only commercial television broadcaster the opportunity provided the companies that then made up the independent television sector with a goldmine of advertising opportunity. As a result the companies that owned the licences to broadcast such as Granada, LWT and TVS were able to sell their advertising spaces quite easily. It was not until 1982 that a second commercial station, Channel 4, came on stream. But C4 was not a real rival to the ITV companies; its special remit from the government was to commission programmes to target minority and alternative audiences. As these audiences would by their very nature be small it was obvious that C4 would have difficulties in attracting large amounts of advertising revenue. The ITV companies were therefore charged with selling C4's advertising in its first years so providing it with a regular income without the concerns of having to attract advertisers by populist programming.

By the mid-80s the ITV companies and the BBC, although in competition for audiences, had created what the government of the day regarded as a 'cosy duopoly'. They rubbed along together quite well both of them having a Public Service remit in some form and neither of them really challenging the other's economic base. This did not sit well with the then Conservative government's ideological stance of privatisation. In the 1990 Broadcasting Act they instigated a process of de-regulation and auctioning of the franchises of the Independent stations. As a result several companies lost their licences to broadcast, such as TVS which was taken over by Meridian. The auction was by sealed bids and the companies had to pay the government money to own the licence.

There were other changes afoot in the broadcasting profile in Britain. Cabling had been progressing slowly but coming up fast was satellite television. There were two companies in operation. Sky, owned by Rupert Murdoch who had set up his production company in Europe (Luxemburg), and BSB, a consortium of companies including ITV companies. Sky had a policy of aggressively selling its dishes and the circle dishes became more prevalent on the skyline than the 'squarials' of BSB. It was obvious that there was not going to be space in the market for both and by dint of relaxing the rules a 'merger' took place and BSkyB was formed.

In 1998 the final terrestrial channel, Channel 5, was launched. This was also a commercial station. In addition C4's position regarding advertising had changed and it had begun selling its own advertising space. So there was more competition for all the companies. In summary, the nineties saw the following:

- the terrestrial television companies having to make more money through advertising before they even began to make programmes;

- an increase in competition for the advertising revenue;

- an ongoing economic fluctuation in business that made expensive television advertising revenue very uncertain.

As a result of all these factors there was a gradual move to consolidate ownership in commercial television. With the additional factor of digital broadcasting, the fragmentation effect on advertising and audiences has yet to be fully judged. Both the BBC and ITV with its Ondigital company were working towards new digital stations. The cost of this development combined with the slowing of advertising revenue left the ITV companies who had backed this development in difficulties. Ondigital collapsed and the two main backers, Granada and Carlton, were forced to consider merging. This happened in February 2004. It meant that the merged company, ITVplc, had 52 per cent of the TV advertising market. Ofcom has lifted the barrier from C4 (which controls about 20 per cent of the market), C5 and BSkyB merging their sales operation, which may have the following effects:

- a lot more sponsorship of programming on terrestrial commercial television;

- greater choice for advertisers of where to place their advertisements;

- targeting of their audience very carefully by advertisers looking at the schedules and the audience profile of all stations before they place an advertisement. This is one of the reasons for the multiplicity of soaps in prime time.

1.6 Television as a medium – time is money

Television is an audio-visual medium. This means it relies on sound and image for its impact. The images and sound of ads have to catch our attention when really we want to watch a programme. They have to sell the idea of the product, they have to leave

NOTES:

us with a message that they hope we will remember whether it's a **slogan**, a **jingle**, an image. It must therefore combine sound and image in a sophisticated way to do all of these in a few seconds.

Slogans can become outdated. Mars dropped its famous 'A Mars a day helps you work, rest and play' in March 2002 after 40 years and replaced it with 'Pleasure you can't measure'. Similarly KitKat has recently changed its slogan from 'Have a break... have a KitKat' to 'Make the most of your break' (*The Independent*, 3 August 2004). Often such a major change is the response to a business crisis.

Television is also a medium that is time specific. What do I mean by that? Everything you see on television travels through time. It doesn't stop unless you hit the pause button or re-wind if it's on a recording. Unlike still images over which we can sit and mull or go back to at a later time and in a different context, television is of the moment. Advertisers have to catch us in that moment in which we are viewing; advertisers only have a few seconds of our time before we are engrossed in the reason why we really turned on the television, be it a soap or a football match. A television advertisement cannot be static, it must move through time. It therefore has **linearity** or a time line. Timing is also important for schedulers and so therefore for advertisers.

1.7 Television scheduling

The average Briton watches 3 hours 41 minutes of television every night ('How Do they Do It?', Taylor, *The Guardian*, 19 November 2002). Scheduling is about maximising your audiences in competition with the other broadcasters. The broadcasting landscape has become much more complex since the 'cosy duopoly' that existed when only BBC and ITV were on the landscape. Now we have satellite, digital, cable as well as terrestrial; and of course computers and mobile phones are providing advertisers with further opportunities to target markets. The web is proving a cheap alternative to target specific and **niche** audiences. **Convergence** means that in future we will be able to get all of these through one screen. Advertisers have to respond to these new technologies as do broadcasters.

The role of the scheduler is to put on programmes that will encourage viewing of their channel rather than that of the competition. Obviously the content of the programme is a major factor – *Teletubbies* has a specific audience and would be unsuitable for broadcasting at 10 p.m.

In the past television was only on for a limited time of day. For example the schedule for ITV-London on Thursday 25 April 1963 (as listed in the *Daily Express*) was as follows:

- start time 2.20 p.m. – racing from Epsom (until 4.30 p.m.);
- 4.30 p.m. onwards – programming for children, family viewing, news, quiz, sitcom, play;
- 9 p.m. news, news review, drama by Alfred Hitchcock, news, documentary;
- finish time 11.40 p.m. – epilogue with The Rev. Dr. Hugh Fearn.

As can be seen the availability of advertising space was much more limited then with only nine hours of broadcasting and a limited resource can always be sold at a premium. Today of course we have almost 24-hour television and for the commercial television stations 24 hours of advertising has to be found to pay for it.

Television has traditionally carved up the schedules into various blocks. For all stations, commercial or not, the most important is **prime time** or **peak time**. This is the period when most people are watching television. It starts around 7 p.m. until about 10.30 p.m., depending on the evening involved. It is also the period that is important for advertisers when the most affluent members of the community, i.e. those who are working, are watching.

The schedulers are not free to just watch the competition. They also have to be aware of other factors, such as the age of their viewers. There is a Family Viewing Policy that regulates the types of programme on at particular times of the day. The BBC and ITV (ITC up to 2003) and Ofcom have all adhered to this policy. This has been partly as a response from pressure groups such as the National Listeners and Viewers Association (NVLA), now known as Mediawatch-uk. Such groups believe that what children and vulnerable people see on television influences them (see media effects in the Glossary). This has meant that there is agreed self-regulation by the broadcasters that anything deemed too 'adult' in content is only broadcast after 9 p.m., often called the '9 o'clock watershed'. After this time it is assumed that parents take on the responsibility for what children see on television.

Advertisers have also had to adhere to these guidelines so that images that might frighten or disturb, or contain inappropriate language or material will not be shown before the watershed. But the carefully constructed Family Viewing Policy appears more and more difficult to sustain within the new multi-channel fragmented landscape. In addition there have been many social changes, not least on what constitutes family viewing given the new family profiles emerging in the twenty-first century. It is also evident that questions of taste and decency are also areas that fluctuate, for example advertising female sanitary wear would not have been allowed on television in its early years. All of these factors have to be taken into account by schedulers and advertisers. Regulation of advertising is discussed in Part 5.

1.8 Television and audiences – who's watching?

It would seem that advertisers are therefore dependent on schedulers. But the relationship is much more complex. Advertisers want stable, reliable and predictable audiences. This suggests that television programming such as soap operas and situation comedies will be popular with advertisers. Advertisers still bid for the prime time slots on television and for other good slots relevant to their products. Schedulers have an eye for their television competitors but also for which programmes will deliver specific audiences to the advertisers. Although audiences could surf the channels at the press of a button, they still tend to stay with one channel over a prolonged period. This is why schedules work on the principles of the inheritance factor, **hammocking, pre-echo, common junction points** and **pre-scheduling** (see Glossary under **schedule**) to capture and keep audiences watching their station.

Advertisers use the British Audience Ratings Bureau (BARB) to find out information on audiences (**demographics**). This organisation provides statistics to the channels and the advertisers telling them who is watching and when. Traditionally this has been partly done by looking at areas such as class. If you remember we said earlier that prime time was an important period for advertisers because that is when the most affluent members of society will be watching. So it is not only a case of *how many* but also *who* is watching. In 1986 the advertising agencies got BARB to split the categories E and D which were then the two categories covering 'the working class' and had been elided by BARB. The reason for this change was that the E category was mainly made up of Old Age Pensioners and the unemployed. They had plenty of time to watch television and therefore viewed lots of adverts; but had very little money to spend on the products being advertised. Advertisers therefore felt that this was skewing the viewing figures, especially during the day, to appear to be advertising to a large number of potential customers. In fact these 'customers' were not at all potential because of age and income.

NOTES:

So advertising and television have a complex symbiotic relationship. Issues of control, regulation and even censorship are evident in the way that television and advertising work in this relationship.

1.9 The key concepts of Media Studies

As a guideline for any study of advertisements there are certain key concepts listed below. These correspond with the separate sections of this book:

- texts – semiotics, narrative and genre (Part2);

- audiences – how they are constructed (Part 3);

- ideology – meanings and representations (Part 4);

- institutions – ownership and who is in control (Part 5).

The key questions to ask therefore are:

- Who made this text?

- Who is it targeted at?

- What is the purpose?

- Who will gain from it?

Conclusion

In the West most people are media literate and gain this literacy by a process of 'osmosis'. Other media forms provide knowledge of narrative and genre codes and conventions and these are appropriated by the advertising industry. They also rely on our cultural and social knowledge. Students will have this background literacy to inform discussions that will bring out many of the points made formally here. They will already be active in understanding texts and enjoy the creativity of many advertising campaigns even if they are not the target audience. The sophistication of their analysis will only be limited by factors such as their lack of cultural reference points and the analytical tools required to decode critically an advertisement's message. The next section provides these tools of analysis.

Activities

Research the History of Advertising

 Go to the ASA web site (www.asa.org.uk) and the schools and colleges section:

- Find out more about the first law suit against an advert with unfounded claims.

- Investigate the Pears Soap advertisement and the Bubbles picture.

- Prepare a short report on early advertising.

Role Playing

 Divide into two groups – the client and the advertising agency. The aim is for the client group to choose a product that is at present in vogue such as a mobile phone or soft drink and for the agency group to develop an advertising campaign for it.

Client Group

Write a proposal (a brief) for an advertising agency to work on in preparing your campaign. Include the following in your proposal:

- product and name;

- target market, e.g. teenage girls;

- unique selling point of product, e.g. mobile phone cases can be changed to fit your handbag;

- line of appeal - fashion, coolness;

- a short profile of the image of the person buying the product.

Agency Group

Use this proposal to develop a storyboard or animatic (with some moving and still images) for the advertisement. Present it for approval to the client.

Reverse the roles so that each group has a chance to produce a campaign and present it for approval.

TV Scheduling and Advertising

 Draw up a schedule for a new imaginary TV station by cut and pasting programmes from a range of television magazines. Separate the slots into breakfast time, children's time, prime time and late night. Justify choice of genres; target audience and suggest possible adverts in breaks.

Advertising and Regulation

 **Task**

Research the Ofcom guidelines -www.ofcom.org.uk

- Choose one specific area to investigate such as alcohol or children.
- Prepare a summary of what you have found to share with your class or group.

Primary Research on Audience and Schedules

Divide into groups within the class.

 **Task**

- Watch a certain number of hours of television from each of the terrestrial commercial television channels. The time slots could be prime time or after school, etc.
- Note adverts shown in between programmes and at breaks.
- Draw up a table of results, like this:

time	programme/genre	target audience	adverts/sponsors

- What scheduling decisions have been made regarding the type of audience?
- What connection can be made between the programmes and the advertisements?
- Were any programmes sponsored?
- What connections could be made between the sponsor and their programme?

Decoding Advertisements

2.1 Introduction: Decoding the message

Young people are avid readers of media and automatically, almost unconsciously, see thousands of advertisements every year. They are also sophisticated consumers of popular culture and this enables advertisers to use this knowledge intertextually as each discourse 'leaks' into the other and the 'message' is read. In order to complete an analysis of complex advertisements with their cultural, social and symbolic references and iconography, you need to develop the skills associated with the study of signs (semiotics) and a methodology to read these signs in a conscious and coherent way. This may sound obvious, but it is worth reminding yourself when presenting texts to readers who unconsciously deconstruct meaning without being able to verbalise how they have achieved this. As in all reading it is essential in deconstructing an advertisement to understand the languages involved.

to identify the elements that construct the advert and more importantly the ideological messages. It is easier to identify elements when more distanced from our own personal consumption. Ideology works by apparently appearing natural, 'just there', obvious, and old advertisements break that 'natural' effect. Students (and teachers) also often have quite a nostalgia and affection for old ads that allow them to reminisce. There are also educational resources available with advertisements on video or CD. There is an American website that has old Coca-Cola television ads (www.memory.loc.gov). Occasionally there are television programmes made of compilations of advertisements, particularly foreign ones. These can also be useful to show cultural differences. The Internet has brand sites such as Coca-Cola and Hewlett Packard where their advertising campaigns are shown. Finally there are the professional sources such as advertising agencies and media houses that will compile a show reel for educational purposes. A list of these and other sources can be found in the Resources section at the back of this book.

2.2 Collecting resources

As it is almost impossible to 'catch' specific television adverts the best method it to record adverts from different channels and time periods over a week. These can then be compiled into different categories and used for individual teaching purposes such as audience segmentation, product comparisons, lines of appeal, messages and meanings and so on. This resource inevitably will 'age' quite rapidly, but this ageing has an invaluable effect as it distances the advertisements from the contemporary and actually helps students

2.3 Analytical tools

Some advertisements are quite simple in that they give very basic information such as what the product is, where to buy it and the cost. These are most usually found in newspaper classified advert columns but rarely on television. Occasionally a local firm will advertise on a regional station for a special promotion, such as a sale, using the informational technique in which a still visual with a voice-over or graphics are used. But most television advertisements involve more complex construction and therefore more sophisticated skills to decode them. It is these types of complex advertisement that will be focused upon.

NOTES:

Semiotics, the science of **signs**, gives us the tools by which we can analyse texts. The basic structure is to look at what you can see or read in terms of all the elements and then how these create meanings individually and collectively, either implicit or explicit. To attempt to begin this on a complex television advertisement would be a skill too far for many readers and it would be beneficial to use still images, such as display advertisements in magazines as an initial introduction to begin this work.

Reading a 'text'

When we read an image we do not go through it in a linear way as with reading a written text. We read holistically and move around in an apparently random way. Although we are being led by the design to look at the key art or other elements first, it is not essential that we do it in a required order to make sense of the image. This means that different readers would give a variety of answers if asked about what was noticed about an advertisement. Therefore a systematic approach helps create a coherent discussion as well as train the readers to work through an advertisement carefully and logically.

It is often possible to say what the advertisement 'means' but not how we got to that conclusion. A superficial reading may miss many of the more subtle messages. The Deconstructing Advertisements activity on pages 24–27 shows how to get to the position whereby readers can analyse television adverts successfully. This will lead the students through a reading of an advert in a structured and active way.

2.4 Television as a medium

Having done at least one analysis with a print product the next stage is to move onto the language of television. The medium of television uses sound and images in combination. To analyse means to take apart this in order to see how the combination works.

The languages used by television advertising are visual, sound, technical and graphics (see activity page 28). The image is moving so it becomes important to isolate certain elements on which to focus each time it is watched. A stepped analysis, as was done with the display advertisements, will make this a coherent process. Segment an advert into scenes or sequences for the students so that they can answer the key questions on each 'language' for each segment as it is played. Printed sheets with the 'elements' for each segment will help the students to identify and analyse more logically following a linear structure. References can then be made forward and backward and between sheets to show how elements work in combination to create a meaning.

What follows is a detailed framework by which students should be able to analyse any advertisements. This is followed by a worked example.

2.5 Technical codes

Lighting and colour (see activity sheet page 29)

Lighting creates atmosphere. **Low key** lighting can create deep shadows which may suggest a sense of danger. Lighting can tell the time of day, or create a sunny, happy feel. Ask the following:

- Is it low key or high key lighting?

- Is it expressionistic with lots of shadows and spot lights, back lighting to give silhouettes?

- Is it apparently natural lighting (remember it will never be totally 'natural') sunny and warm, cool and dark? Does the lighting reflect the weather, time of day?

- What does the lighting say about the advertisement and the product?

- Does the lighting fit into a convention such as a genre?

Colours can signify such things as the time of year (as when leaves are green). They can suggest warmth or coolness depending on what side of the colour spectrum they lie. In addition they have cultural meanings. In the West the colour of mourning is black but this does not hold for Eastern countries where white is often used. In the West the bride is often in white, signifying purity and innocence. In India red is the bridal colour. If a woman is dressed in red in this country there are usually different connotations. Colour is also psychological. Dark colours 'feel' heavier than light colours, for example.

Decoding Advertisements

Sound (see activity sheet page 30)

'Happiness is a cigar called Hamlet'

The sounds we hear can often tell us a lot more than we realise. If you tried to listen to a short extract of a film without the visuals you may be surprised how much you can hear and read from the sounds such as of cars driving on a road or feet crunching on sand. Sounds give lots of information almost without us realising. Asking questions about sound in adverts can be difficult in that you cannot point to the element in discussion. A discussion could focus around such areas as:

- Is there music? What is the style (soft and lyrical, harsh; martial, etc.)?

- What instruments are used, e.g. brass or strings? What atmosphere is created, e.g. military or romantic?

- What melody is used? Is it well known or not? Is it classical or popular? Hamlet cigars famously used 'Air on a G-String' for a series of advertisements.

- Does the music indicate a particular place or country? For example, an accordion often signifies France whilst brass band-style signifies the North of England.

- Voices: consider the gender used, the accent and dialect; the style of voice – fast and furious, low and sexy; the tone – angry, friendly (see also Part 2.8 for further work on accents and dialects).

- Is there ambient sound to suggest the general location, such as the wind in trees and birds for a country location?

- What is the use of sound effects and how do they help tell the narrative, such as a clock or a bell to indicate time or place?

Camera (see activity sheet page 31)

Everything is constructed and storyboarded before it is filmed. The choice of the camera frame, the focus and the movement are important as they will convey meaning. The camera is part of the action, not an unbiased observer. Consider how subjective the camera is in any advert you are analysing – does it make you feel part of the action or a bystander observing? This position might change several times in an advert. Sometimes you could be placed in the position of one of the characters by a point of view (POV) shot and then move to a bird's eye view looking down on the action.

- Cameras can focus on a very small area (big close up – BCU) through to a wide expanse (extreme long shot – ELS).

- A camera can choose to concentrate on a small aspect or wander around.

- A camera is static or mobile (pan, track, tilt, dolly, arc and crane). All of which create meaning. Choice is important.

- The camera can also provide meaning through angle. A low angle (LA) will make the subject look powerful and the reverse with a high angel (HA), although be wary as this reading does not always work. It can be canted or tilt and create distortion (*The Third Man*, 1949, uses this 'Dutch angle' frequently).

- In addition the camera can move, tilting up and down, panning left and right, tracking something and swirling around a subject.

- There are also handheld and other movements possible. All of which create a dynamic feel to an image.

- The focus may change from the background, pulled to the foreground to make the audience look at something, such as the product, and leaving the background out of focus. It can keep both foreground and background in focus – this is called

NOTES:

deep focus (famously used to great effect in *Citizen Kane*, 1941).

There are many textbooks and websites that give glossaries with explanations and examples of framings and camera movements (see Resources).

Editing

Having filmed the footage, it has to be edited together. When moving from one frame to another you can choose to cut, dissolve, to use a wipe, and so on. The effects will be different so watch the transitions carefully when studying and ask yourself why they occurred:

- some editing will allow you to forget that it has been edited through a clever use of continuity effect;

- other editing will be so fast and furious or unusual that the montage will be obvious. What is the effect of montage editing? It can create fear or excitement, it can be used to deliver a lot of information rapidly or be used to create a social or political statement by the clever use of **juxtaposition**.

Special effects

These could include animation, CGI (computer generated imagery), the change of colour from monochrome to psychedelic, posterisation, **slomo**, and so on. If you noticed the use of a special effect, ask why the effect has been used. Does it, for example, help to tell the story or to create a generic style?

There are other factors that can contribute to adverts depending upon their style. Genre and narrative are important elements in many television adverts as are the use of language, the mode of address and graphics.

2.6 Graphics and language

Although graphics are not often used in television adverts they will appear as a logo or a slogan. It is therefore worth looking at the style of the print – whether it is informal or formal, does it look like handwriting, is it strong and bold or is it fluid and feminine? Does it convey a period, such as Gothic font? All these may add to your understanding of

the meaning of the advertisement. Again this is difficult to gather using moving images but it is possible to find such examples from the parallel campaigns being run in magazines and display advertisements. What do the words convey? Is punctuation used and why? Is there the use of **ellipse** (a gap in time) for example for the reader to fill? What words are being spoken? What do they connote? Are there puns used? Are there superlatives, e.g. 'the best…'? Is alliteration used? Does the language used suggest beliefs or ideas? Does it use the imperative verb form; 'Go to work on an egg'?

Narrative (see activity sheet page 32)

Most advertisements tell or imply a 'story' in their brief time slot. Very few adverts use surreal techniques with anti-narrative devices (such as in the 'Dolphin' advert for Guinness or the Silk Cut cigarette adverts).

As in all narratives an advert will be full of ellipses to condense the story that the reader is expected to fill in mentally. The advert will also go through time and space, not just the actual time of the advert, but also the imagined time of the narrative, and different spatial positions will be adopted to help create the narrative.

A narrative may only be implicit, but often you can re-constitute it from very little information. Sometimes the advert will signal an ongoing story such as the famous Nescafé Gold Blend that used this device very successfully in a romantic/soap style of adverts over a period of time. Other ongoing narratives using the same characters were run by the 'Katy' adverts for OXO and the Nicole/Papa ads for Renault cars.

A narrative will be mainly told through images but the soundtrack, with sound effects, voice-over and dialogue will be used to help fill the gaps or ellipses. Music could be used to suggest elements such as atmosphere or place.

There are many theories about how narratives work, such as Propp, Todorov, Lévi-Strauss and Barthes. If you want to read further into narrative look in text books such as *The Media Students Book* (Branston and Stafford, 2001). Here are listed some key factors which can help to analyse how a narrative works:

Decoding Advertisements

Key characters in a narrative may take on certain functions (a la Propp), such as:

- Protagonists (heroes and heroines);

- Antagonists (villains);

- Wise person;

- Blocker;

- Helper.

There will be a series of events to help the narrative along.

Action events work with enigma events (questions, such as, What will happen?) to move the narrative along (as with Barthes' primary codes). There will be codes of dress to identify class, age, occupation and so on, of the characters. The **non verbal communication** (NVC) of the actors will be important in telling the story. This includes not only the way they behave and look but also how they are *put together*. There might be symbolic elements that convey meaning such as a flag to identify a country and cultural signs that signify important information in the narrative (Barthes' secondary codes). Time and space can be manipulated as in flashbacks or camera cuts and our narrative viewpoint can change (see Todorov). We can read the narrative through **binary oppositions** such as good and bad, cool or un-cool consumer (Lévi-Strauss).

There are types of narrative that are popular with adverts, such as:

- the presenter style where an actor directly addresses the consumer about the product and often demonstrates the benefits of the product;

- the **slice of life** ad, in which we eavesdrop onto an apparently real conversation;

- the testimonial from a famous person so that the product is linked to the person as in the L'Oreal ads ('**because you're worth it**');

- the problem that can be solved - miraculously!

- the 'before' and 'after' narrative showing the benefits of the product or service;

- moral stories, such as car insurance or car aid;

- the puzzle of how something was achieved;

- the joke with the punch-line at the end.

Further types can be found on agency web sites and in Greg Myers' *Ad Worlds*, (1999).

Genre (see activity sheet page 33)

Closely linked to narrative is the concept of genre. We referred to the romantic soap genre of the Gold Blend advert which was aimed at a female target audience interested in the romantic genre and who were the purchasers of coffee.

Discuss

a) What were women buying when they bought this brand of coffee?

b) Are there genres referenced in current television advertisements?

Genre means a *type* of story, such as horror. Horror can be sub-divided, for example into 'slasher' horror or Gothic horror, as in vampire stories. Would horror be a good genre to sell a product? If so, what type of product and to what type of audience would this appeal? Churchyards and gravestones were used in the AIDS campaign ads in the early 1990s. Parody of the horror genre has also been used.

NOTES:

How do you spot the genre? This is done through generic **codes** and **conventions**. It might be a very obvious icon such as the vampire teeth, or a more subtle convention such as low-key lighting with deep shadows, perhaps reminiscent of German Expressionism.

What is important to remember is that genre only works because we know about the codes and conventions. We are media literate and we have cultural knowledge. The advertisers have to rely upon this for the advertisement to work.

Mise-en-scène

The way we understand the narrative and genre is partly through the way that each shot is composed and laid out within the frame. Look at the composition of each frame and what elements are in it. Look at the key art – the most important aspect of the image – and then look around the key art at the **mise-en-scène** (this is a term used with film which means everything that makes meaning inside the frame).

- What other things help to tell the narrative – maybe a picture on a wall?

- Where is it set? Country, rural, urban, suburban, city?

- What is in the background to suggest the setting and any other elements that seem important?

- How are the objects and characters arranged in the frame? Are they near or far? Close together or separated by a table indicating a split in relationship? To use *Psycho* (1960) as an example, if you watch the parlour scene you will see how director Alfred Hitchcock carefully places the birds in the frame to comment upon the characters of Norman and Marion.

This leads to the final element that is significant in an advert.

Intertextuality

Another way advertisers use the consumer's own knowledge is to reference other texts. This can be done to transfer the values of the other text to the product, to make a joke, to make us take notice, to make us feel clever. The advertisers are drawing on our textual knowledge to help them sell. This is called **intertextuality**. One effect of this technique is to create adverts that are sometimes called postmodern in style. That is, they reference many forms of popular culture in an eclectic range with apparently little coherence. It is said by theorists to reflect the instability of culture in a globalisation of capital with the effect in localisation of identity. It is a style often used in music videos with its emphasis on fragmentation.

So the signs, the signifiers, do not have a single meaning but are free to make new meanings in their new context as well as referencing the old. This can be seen in the Punk safety-pin fashion, for example which was again re-worked by Versace for the famous Liz Hurley dress. Advertising is particularly vulnerable to intertextuality because it draws on popular culture to make its meaning. The advertising world will take from culture what it believes will capture the attention of the audience and then feed it back re-worked. So Hamlet cigars' use of 'Air on a G–String'; Guinness's use of surreal art; and the monster horror genre utilised in a throat lozenge campaign. Actual films such as *Casablanca* (1942), *The Blues Brothers* (1980) and *King Kong* (1933) as well as genres have been invoked in adverts. Ford appropriated and re-worked the chase sequence from *Bullitt* (1968) for its Puma ads in the 1990s.

There have been accusations that the advertising industry is poaching the work of other artists. Magnum, an agency which represents photographers, has accused the advertising industry of plagiarising photographer's work. For example Young and Rubicam, one of Britain's biggest agencies, paid compensation to a leading American photographer Elliot Erwitt over a Hush Puppy ad ('Snap! Ad agencies caught using copycat photographs', Hindle, *The Sunday Times*, 6 November, 1994). In a further postmodern twist some adverts will parody other ads (as Irn-Bru parodied a Coke campaign).

Why should advertisers do this? Are they just lazy or uninventive? Probably not – what they are doing is delving into our image bank and seeing with what associations or connotations these images are connected. So a piece of fine art may have images of wealth, of sophistication and so on. These then become connected with the product being sold. For Punk, of course, it was the opposite – the connection was with rubbish in order to be iconoclastic. This form of appropriating and using other discourses was termed **bricolage** by Lévi-Strauss. For the link to be made in terms of the transfer of meaning the work has to be done by the reader of the text. In actual fact it is probably more often quite unconscious references that are made rather than purposeful and conscious links by the advertiser. Judith Williamson (1978) talks about the 'overt' and the 'latent' meaning of an advertisement. In order for the latent meaning to be triggered the knowledge – cultural, social or, in Barthes' terms, the mythic – has to be within the reader so that the significance is transferred from this knowledge to the product being sold. Intertextuality is the use either consciously or unconsciously of material from other texts, and so meaning is generated by references from these interactions in a postmodern style.

2.7 Brands – 'A rose by any other name ...' (see activity sheet page 34)

Why do we buy brands? Why buy a Rolex even if it is from a dodgy market stall? What are you buying as well as the brand?

What do you get with a Rolex watch? Is it the James Bond/Pierce Bronson image and the lifestyle associated with both the real and fictional characters? With the brand you are buying status, power, success, national pride and sexual appeal. Or at least that is what the advertisers hope that the branding will indirectly suggest.

In the research on markets brand name identity is seen to be an important part of the image that people buy. Brand identity is made up of a combination of factors. These are its personality and its values. Does it have a past, a story, a history? How does it look? What is its iconicity? What would be its likes and dislikes? What emotional benefits will it provide and what are the listed benefits such as size, efficiency and cost? How can all these be summed up in a single sentence for the advertiser and how can this be converted into a single slogan for the market? Brands such as Hovis bread have presented themselves as part of the heritage of traditional food, of a traditional way of life with all those 'good' qualities that they represent. Its personality has been of wholeness and goodness. It has provided untainted food and it is these values which makes Hovis 'the brand' and which have been represented in the television adverts such as the famous one where a delivery boy with old fashioned bicycle struggles up a cobbled street delivering bread that has just been locally baked. All this was shot in sepia tones to connote an old photographic image and sustain the myth of home or local baking.

Branding is something of a minefield for producers as well as purchasers. If a brand becomes associated with something negative it can be its nemesis. During the period when the AIDS crisis was just becoming a public health crisis in the

NOTES:

United Kingdom there was also a slimming brand called Aids. It was not a good brand name to have for a product aimed at getting people to lose weight. Trying to keep a brand name clean is important for the manufacturers. Recently Coca-Cola has had to deal with the publicity associated with its new bottled water product, Dasani. This was identified as being basically filtered tap water and gave the impression that Coca-Cola was 'cheating' its customers. Following a testing failure the product has been withdrawn in the UK. Will it be re-branded? Other brands such as Nike have been associated with exploiting Third World workers and have had to rigorously prove their status as caring employers. In contrast the Co-Op has built its brand on supporting Fair Trade and is attracting consumers such as 'Reformers' (see Part 3 on Audiences)

Douglas Rushkoff in an article in *The Times* 2000 – see www.pbs.org: 'A Brand by Any Other Name') tells the story of a boy standing in front of a range of trainers unable to make a choice because 'I don't know which of these trainers is me'. The Nike trainers were possibly too anti-green; Airwalk were also too large a company; others were too 'hip' for his current school persona; and the retro brands such as Puma were not his era. He was stumped.

2.8 Language and voices

'Words, words words' (Hamlet)

But words are rarely neutral and voices are certainly not. In this country we tend to place values onto accents and dialects, often depending upon the area in which we live. In advertising, Received Pronunciation (RP accent) is generally assumed to have the highest status, but it may not appeal to everyone, for example a young audience who may prefer a regional or mid-Atlantic accent connected with the current popular cultural trends. If there is a strong rural regional accent, as in the Hovis ad with its northern accented **voice-over** it can signify warmth, trustworthiness and integrity. Certain foreign accents can be used to suggest certain values. For example, a French or German accent may have different connotations. An American accent could suggest a certain modernity or popular cultural references. The gender of the voice is also significant as is the pitch.

Most voice-overs are male – ask yourself why. What is the value implicit in the male voice? In addition voices have been 'coloured' by advertising agencies in order to classify them. A deep bass tone is given the colour dark chocolate brown. Brian Glover the actor who provided the voice-over for the Tetley Tea Folk had this colour of voice. What colour would you associate with the film trailers which use a particular male American voice: 'Coming soon to this cinema'?

Whilst the style in which the words are said can help to influence meaning, the actual words can **anchor** images into a specific meaning. In the Hall Agency advert for East Kilbride (see activity sheets pages 77–78) it is the words of the song, 'Around the world …' which help to anchor the meaning of the advert to the various places around the globe we see referenced visually.

Words themselves have values attached. You could, for example, have a *horse*, a *steed* or a *nag*. Which of these would you prefer to have if you were a horse owner? So while analysing an advert, do not forget about the words they speak as well as style, accent, dialect, tone, gender, age and 'colour' of the voices used.

Conclusion

Advertisements are complex texts. In this section we have looked at the many elements that go into the construction of a television advertisement. In order to become a skilled deconstructor of a TV advert it is necessary to practise using techniques such as those suggested. The activities associated with this section have been designed to facilitate a coherent methodology for analysis. Do not be fooled into thinking that the advert 'just happened'. They cost a lot of money to make and everything, but everything, must contribute to the message.

Deconstructing Advertisements

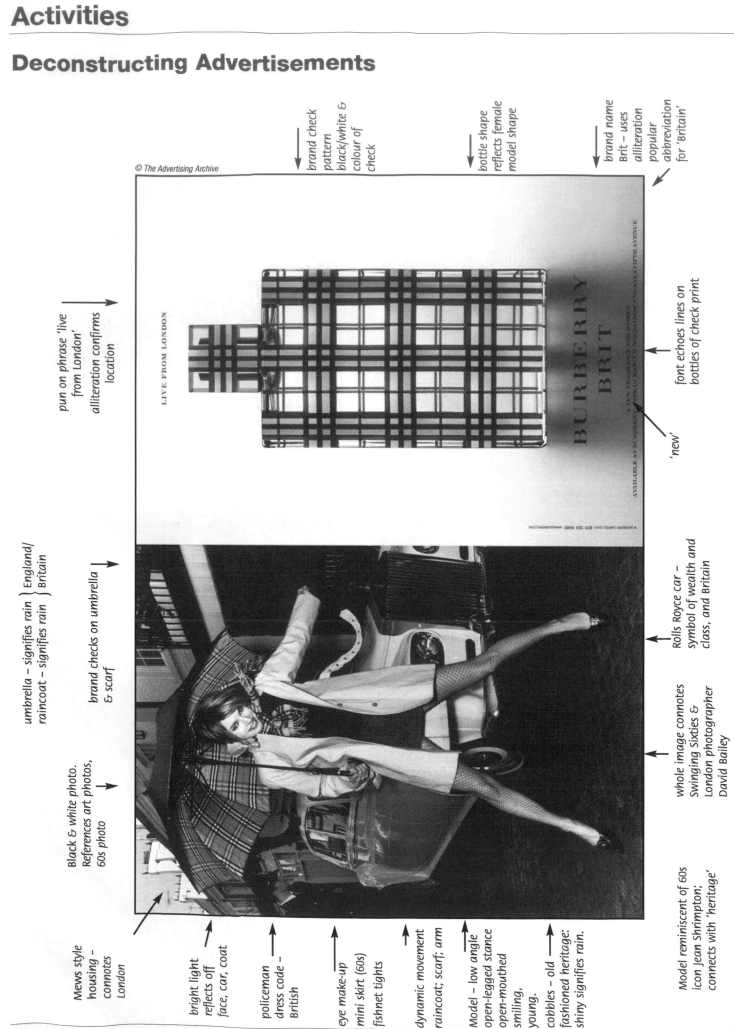

brand check pattern black/white & colour of check

bottle shape reflects female model shape

brand name Brit – uses alliteration popular abbreviation for 'Britain'

pun on phrase 'live from London' alliteration confirms location

font echoes lines on bottles of check print

'new'

umbrella – signifies rain } England/Britain
raincoat – signifies rain } Britain

brand checks on umbrella & scarf

Rolls Royce car – symbol of wealth and class, and Britain

whole image connotes Swinging Sixties & London photographer David Bailey

Black & white photo. References art photos, 60s photo

Mews style housing – connotes London

bright light reflects off face, car, coat

policeman dress code – British

eye make-up mini skirt (60s) fishnet tights

dynamic movement raincoat; scarf; arm

Model – low angle open-legged stance open-mouthed smiling, young.

cobbles – old fashioned heritage: shiny signifies rain.

Model reminiscent of 60s icon Jean Shrimpton; connects with 'heritage'

© The Advertising Archive

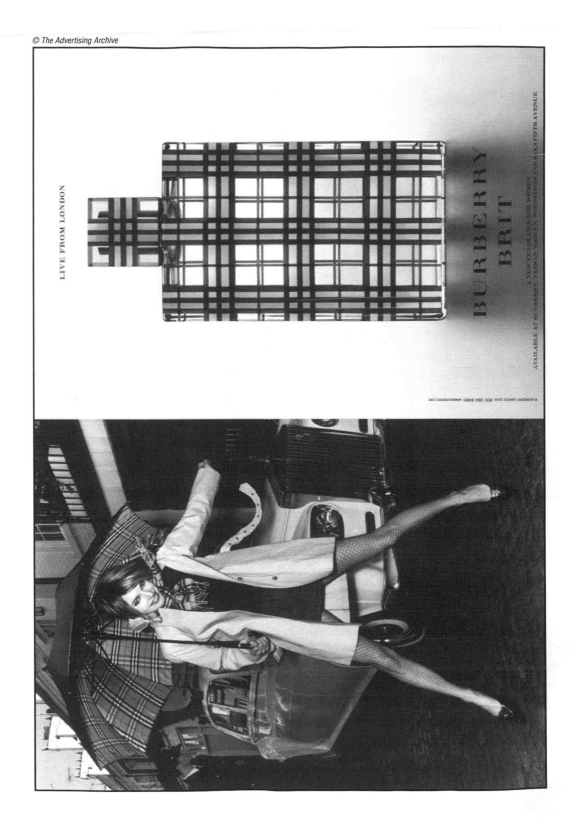

Burberry Brit Perfume

Write a list of words on left side with space on right to fill in a chart to analyse this advert

Elements	Connotations/Significance/Meanings
Location	
Car	
Policeman	
Woman: stance, dress, NVC, objects	
Technical codes: camera angle, lighting, colour	
Bottle	
Captions (language and font)	
Brand name	
Product name	
Intertextuality	
Meanings and myths	

Deconstructing Advertisements – Teacher Notes

- First show a worked example of an analysis with elements, denotation and connotation filled in.

- Follow this example with a group/class analysis worked together. This can be done as a paper exercise, OHP or power point. Show an advert. Give a list of elements seen in the advert in a column (related to people, objects, colour, camera angles, lighting, composition as in the worked example) and next to it a column for the meaning or connotations. This exercise should reveal a mainly agreed 'preferred' reading of the advertisement's meaning and show how individuals read adverts in a similar way. However discussion might reveal alternative views or a 'negotiated' reading.

- An individual/paired exercise follows where the students are given a specific advert to label and analyse but with some guidance as to what elements should be put in the columns and discussed.

- Finally students use their own advertisement. They should paste the A4 adverts onto a larger sheet of paper, then draw lines to each of the elements and explain the connotation of each. This exercise could focus upon a particular product such as cars; perfumes; mobile phones; trainers. By doing this you will build a resource for later discussion and work to compare different lines of appeal and brands.

- Extension work: Write a paragraph about the advertisement asking 'What is being sold?' 'Who is the target audience?' 'How do you know this from the advertisement?' 'What is the evidence?' 'What do you think the advertiser is really selling; i.e. what is the line of appeal?' In order to get to this stage it is important to have introduced at a basic level the key concepts of target audiences and lines of appeal discussed in Part 3 as well as messages and meanings discussed in Part 4.

Television Language

Task What is a television advertisement made up of? List all the elements that make up an advertisement:

• Action (what happens; narrative);

• Visuals (colour, lighting, camera movements, focus, people and objects, the composition – mise-en-scène);

• Editing (montage, continuity editing, cuts, dissolves, wipes, fades);

• Sounds (voices, dialogue, sound effects, music);

• Graphics (words printed, logos, brand names, print styles).

Lighting and its Meanings

 Draw an object or a face or a figure in the space below. Put an arrow towards it from where the source of light would come. Use a pencil/crayon to mark in the shadows. Say what the effect is on the meaning of the face. For example a face wearing a hat and top lit would have deep shadows over the eyes. What would that say about the person?

The Bells, the Bells

 You are collating a CD-ROM on sound effects for an advertising agency. List as many different types of bells as you can for the recorder to get to put on the CD-ROM – such as typewriter bell, funeral bell, school bell, and so on. Try to get at least 30 bells.

Now show how at least five of the bells could be used in an advertisement for a new soft drink or any other product. For example, a young woman is woken by her <u>alarm bell</u> (signifies early morning) and realises she is going to be late. She rushes past the <u>telephone as it rings</u> (signifies someone is trying to reach her) and dashes out of the house just as the <u>church clock rings</u> the hour (signifies time is passing). As she catches a taxi her <u>mobile rings</u> (signifies urgency) and a message says 'Where are you?' We see her entering a lift and the <u>lift bell</u> rings on the top floor (signifying the end of the journey). She runs out to arrive at a registry office where her best friend is getting married (<u>wedding bells</u> on tape recorder signify marriage has happened). Slogan – *'Don't be the bridesmaid all the time be on time with the handheld organiser from...'*.

Yes, I know it's corny, but this should give you the idea of how and why sound effects are really important.

Hearing is Seeing

Task Listen to several television adverts without the visuals. What information do you hear? List them under the following headings:

- musical style;
- musical instruments;
- ambient sound;
- voices (gender, accent, tone, dialect, style);
- sound effects.

What information has been conveyed aurally?

Now watch the adverts again. Do the visuals confirm your ideas?

Editing Styles

 Watch advertisements and count up how many edit cuts you can see.

What was the ratio of cuts to seconds for the adverts you studied?

Did any adverts have only a few or very many? What were the reasons for these differences? Was it the product?

What style was used – continuity editing (as in the Hollywood style storytelling) or montage editing (as in a pop video or an action sequence)?

Were there special transitions? Why were they used?

Activities

Narrative – Teacher Notes

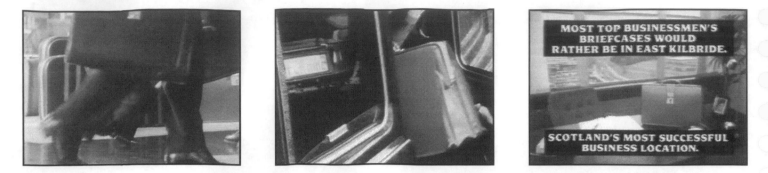

Record an advert that has an obvious storyline but one that doesn't have any strong clues as to its product. The ad from which the above images are taken featured a briefcase travelling around the world. The soundtrack was 'Around the World …in gay Paris and even London Town…'. As you can imagine, as these words were sung signifiers of place, such as a London taxi cab, were shown. The suitcase was carried by a man whose face we never saw. What was the advert selling? A suitcase range? A travel firm? It is not until the end that the viewer discovers the ad is promoting East Kilbride as a business centre.

Having recorded an advertisement that has a narrative but where the product can be easily disguised, write a summary of the action rather like a storyboard – if artistic you can draw this to hand to the students who will see the advert. This could be done as group work. Play the ad without the sound and with no logo or obvious product and ask the students to write a potential storyline from this visual material alone. Also ask if they can tell what is being sold (if the advert is ambiguous like the suitcase advert all the better).

Then hand around a printed version of the soundtrack with each section of music or dialogue transcribed onto a separate strip of paper. The students then have to match the soundtrack to the visuals and the narrative they proposed.

Compare the options proposed with the original. Are the narratives similar? Did the advertisement work? Did you need the soundtrack? What did it add to the narrative? Was there a preferred reading of the advert?

2.6.2 Genre

- List as many genres as you can very quickly.

- Draw a chart with the genres listed down one column. Draw three more columns, like the chart below.

- Observe over a weekend how many genres you can spot in adverts and list them in the second column.

- What are they selling? List the product and its brand name in the third column.

- Who do you think is the target audience? Put this in the fourth column.

Genres	TV ad genres	product/brand	target audience

Culture and Ads

 In the TV advertisements that you are studying how many can you find which refer to other forms of culture, such as radio, television, comics, photography, as well as film, art and music?

Activities

Brands

 Answer the following questions:

- what brands do you buy?;

- why do you buy them?;

- what brands appear in your house?;

- what personalities do brands have?;

- why do some products have to be re-branded?

 Look at the brand of a popular product and see how it matches the criteria identified by Mud Valley, a UK-based brand marketing company:

1. A central organising thought – a one sentence definition.

2. A slogan defining it for the customer.

3. A personality – what would it be like if it was human?

4. Its value - what does it stand for?

5. Its tastes/appearance.

6. Its heritage – what are the stories about it?

7. Its emotional benefits.

8. Its hard benefits.

Adapted from www.mudvalley.co.uk

Language and Voices – Accents and Dialects

Task • Listen to a range of regional accents without any visuals. How do you judge them for their friendliness, honesty, intelligence? If you do this as a class activity is there agreement about their 'value'?

• Listen to a range of female and male voices. What colour would you give each of them? What do the colours signify for you with reference to the voices?

• Write down the scripted words in an advert, either dialogue or voice-over. What is the style of voice(s) used? How does it reflect the message of the advert?

• From the script underline any emotive words. What do these words suggest about the product? Are there any superlatives used or other linguistic devices such as alliteration, puns, similes and metaphors? What other techniques are used such as direct address 'you'? Are words such as 'handmade' used that suggest a value? Or uniqueness such as 'only' suggested? Are there frequently used words to give the message?

Task From the following products, list what kind of voices you think might be most appropriate to use in advertising – mention gender, age, accent and dialect, tone and colour:

• mobile phone;
• insurance company;
• washing powder;
• computer;
• video game;
• trainer;
• hair shampoo;
• cheese;
• high powered car.

Audiences, Research and Targeting

Discuss

What brand names today can stand for the generic product name?

3.1 Why does advertising work?

> '**Advertising is the rattling of a stick inside a swill bucket**' George Orwell

As Orwell's comment suggests, advertising has been around forever. Whenever someone had something to sell they would advertise it somehow, whether it was a barber's pole or the pawnbroker's three balls outside medieval shops, or just someone shouting their wares in the street as portrayed in the musical *Oliver!* (1968).

Today advertising has a far more sophisticated approach to the target market. One aspect is to give a product a brand name that the audience can remember and associate with that product. Some marketing campaigns have been so successful that the brand names became synonymous with the products, such as Hoover and Biro.

The sophistication of identifying markets and targeting them has been the most important change in advertising since Orwell's swill bucket days. Market research has enabled advertising agencies to draw up a series of methods by which they can identify and develop markets. Once identified, advertising agencies hope to develop a need in the target audience for their products. People do have general needs, such as food to keep alive and soap to keep clean. But whereas they do *need* to eat they do not *need* deodorant to smell clean. In fact 50 years ago very few people felt the need to buy deodorant. It was not until a television campaign where a person turned away with wrinkled nose from someone and a 'friend' of the offending person whispered the phrase '*BO*' (body odour) in their ear, thus telling them about their 'problem', that this need was aroused in the public. The solution was not to have a good wash, but to buy deodorant: but which deodorant? Obviously the one that stopped that awful BO! But then wouldn't it be 'cissy' for men to use deodorant that after all was a bit like scent that only women used? Brut solved the problem with its aggressive image personified by the male model. 'As an account executive for a men's aftershave advertisement put it, the product "created the market, or rather, satisfied a need that was already there"' (Davis and Walton 1983).

Having established the need, the decision to buy one brand over another was what the advertisers had to work on. Earlier scientific divisions of markets gave way to the more sophisticated psychological research methods. These told advertisers about the importance of association and about creating a positive image around a product or brand.

3.2 Lines of appeal

'Naughty but nice.'

Advertisers are advised by research to concentrate on the emotional aspect associated with a product. The campaigns that sell dreams and aspirations or work on fears or use any of the other lines of appeal or techniques successfully will help the product to survive in the marketplace. The costs are high but so are the stakes.

Several emotions have been linked with advertising campaigns. The following are some of these:

- greed;
- fear of social non-conformity;
- getting it both ways;
- being the good egg;
- snob appeal/class identification;
- nostalgia;
- fear of loneliness, rejection, incompetence.

Just to take the last – fear – as an example. This winter (2003/4) a campaign for a flu/cold drug, Lemsip, has been running. A businessman with a bad cold is rung up and told by his overlarge boss that if he doesn't get the business there will be difficulties. The man fearing the loss of his job takes the special flu formula and 'hey presto', ('the magic formula', Williamson, 1978) he's better and got the business. Any person who is concerned about their employment, even subconsciously, will perhaps be encouraged a) to struggle into work with a cold and b) to buy the miraculous cure. This is how 'fear' can work in advertising.

Discuss

Do you think this advertisement would have contravened the ITC (now Ofcom) rule 'Advertisements must not without justifiable reason play on fear' (ITC rule no. 16, 'Appeals to Fear')?

Do you know of any advertisements that currently appeal to fear?

Is the appeal to fear more acceptable in the context of public information campaigns or not?

Certainly campaign advertisements and public service advertising do regularly appeal through fear. For example, fear of the consequences of drinking and driving or of unprotected sex. The early AIDS campaign ads, with their images of death through tombstones and horror film lighting, were a clear example of this technique. Examples around drink-drive advertising regularly appear around Christmas, whilst anti-smoking and drugs campaigns also use this line of appeal.

Another very strong line of appeal is that of sex. Here the product is linked by suggestion or implication to sexual appeal. If there was a *direct* link made then there would be issues of censorship and the regulatory authorities (Ofcom and ASA) would be involved, not to mention pressure groups such as Mediawatch-uk. The ASA Schools and Colleges Resources Section 2 'Taste and Decency' has examples of print adverts (see Resources). One classic example of how sex can be implied was the Cadbury flake advertisements. Here a young attractive women unwrapped a Cadbury Flake and pushed it voluptuously into her mouth. The link between the flake and sexual activity was suggested but never explicit and children would have been able to watch the advertisement without understanding the sexual subtext aimed at adults.

Researching the effect

Advertisers know that an audience has made the link between the message and the product through the use of research and by watching the sales figures closely to see the effectiveness of the campaign. In addition they may hold focus groups to collect further anecdotal evidence. The sophisticated link through the construction

The Donor's autumn 2001 issue featured an article outlining the National Blood Service's then current advertising campaign

Audiences, Research and Targeting

Discuss

Think about this question: the story of advertising soap powder is a story of changing roles of women – or is it?

of the image and its message relies upon the understanding of the audience. Nothing is left to chance and at each stage a campaign is tested. The Tetley Tea bag was put under scrutiny as the advertising agency researched whether to change the campaign. There is little difference between one ordinary tea bag and another so the advertisers had to create that difference. The campaign had to give the purchaser something other than a teabag. For Tetley it was the number of perforations, the warmth of the characters of the Tetley Tea Folk connoted by their 'northernness' and comedy associations with them (*Education and Communication*, EH207 TV6 O.U.). PG Tips, meanwhile, had their domesticated chimps, whilst other tea selling points were different teabag shapes.

3.3 Television advertisements and the audience

'For mash get Smash'

As you have read there are many different types of advertisement but we can make some general comments about television advertising and audiences:

- television adverts do not contain much information;

- they do tell us a lot about the target market;

- they have to link in with messages for the same product in other media such as display advertisements in magazines, publicity sites, and radio advertising for the same message;

- repetition is important;

- if the message is changed and a new campaign is launched the message needs reinforcing. Repetition helps this;

- advertising on television is very expensive and this must be taken into account in a marketing campaign as it will influence the cost of the product in the market;

- advertisements on television must use sound and images and develop through time to tell their message.

Audiences in the past

Adverts from the past quite clearly do not work today on modern audiences except perhaps through nostalgia. Soap

powder is a good example. Soap powders have been using broadcasting advertising for many years. The reason why we term on-going stories such as *EastEnders* as 'soap operas' is partly explained by the fact that the earliest incarnation of these dramas were broadcast on radio in America. Soap powders sponsored these shows which were targeted at women at home in the afternoon and so they became known as soap operas (operas because they used very melodramatic storylines such as you find in operas) or now just 'soaps'. Proctor and Gamble first did this with the *Ma Perkins* show. Two of the first advertisements when commercial television started in the UK in 1955 were for washing powder, Surf and Lux (although the very first was for Gibbs SR toothpaste). Today we have washing soap in all sorts of forms and packages – but has the message changed? Have the methods changed? If they haven't – why not?

Early soap powder advertisements on television often followed a formula. This was of two women comparing their washing results. One would have whiter washing than the other. Good friend/neighbour/ mother/wiser woman with the whiter wash then lets out the secret that she uses brand X and she wouldn't swap her brand for two of the other. This formula of 'two women in the kitchen' was repeated constantly (there are less salubrious terms for this formula). So formulaic and banal was this type of advertising to women for soap powders and other goods that David Ogilvy wrote in 1963; 'The consumer isn't a moron, she's your wife.' Other campaigns focused on sending the family out in shirts whiter than white, or getting 'a square deal', or fear of the neighbours seeing underarm stains, or less work for more effect, or making washing a pleasure rather than a chore. As the century ended even a skinhead teenage lad could have a go at washing a shirt (a Unilever campaign).

'New! Improved!' 1950s ad for Daz

'Persil Washes Whiter…'

Today advertising for soap powders in a post-feminist and revisionist era still appears to fall into the formula of women talking about soap and comparing washes. (Most recently the actresses from the sit-com *Birds of a Feather* used an updated form of this formula.) Researchers claim that women approve of this formula. They claim that this is because women feel that their power in the kitchen is being eroded and they need to get back in control. This theory was suggested by research done by Culture Imprint, a research company into consumer behaviour. What do you think?

3.4 Split audiences

As we have said the advertisement has to target the market. But how do you find this market? This is where the advertising agencies use research, sociological, economic and psychological. Historically the class groupings of A, B, C1, C2, D and E (the Registrar General's old scale) were used. Recently these have been superseded by different categories but the general point is that society is broken up into groups by education and income. The highest group has people such as doctors, lawyers (A or 1 in the new category); the middle group has teachers and nurses (B); the next group are the lower managerial and clerical workers (C1); then skilled and semi-skilled manual workers (C2); the unskilled manual workers (D), and finally the unemployed and OAPs (E). But for advertisers who are designing advertisements to appeal to our inner desires and thoughts this is a rather crude division. There have been other groups suggested. One of these was put forward by the agency Young and Rubicam. They divided people into four groups. Firstly, **Mainstreamers**, who make up 40% of the population, and who like security, and belonging to a group. They do not want to stand out from a crowd and will buy branded goods from well-known high street names. Secondly, there are **Aspirers**, who want status and the esteem of others. They like status symbols such as designer labels and expensive watches, and they live off credit and cash. Thirdly, there are **Succeeders**, people who have already got status and control. They do not need status symbols but they need to feel in control all the time, if they are with a group they want to be in charge. Finally, there are the **Reformers**. They define themselves by their self-esteem and self-fulfilment. Status symbols such as designer labels would not

appeal. They are the most highly educated and they often influence new trends in society such as buying own brands, Fair Trade and organic foods.

There are also other ways of categorising people. Sometimes acronyms are used such as **yuppies** (young up and coming urban professionals and executives) and nicknames such as **empty-nesters** (older married people whose children have grown up and left the 'nest'). Today our every purchase is scrutinised. The use of loyalty cards, the Internet and mobile phones have allowed companies unprecedented access to our habits, lifestyles and through psychological profiling our inner needs. Are you 'a clever capitalist, a rising materialist, a bijou home-owner, or a member of the chattering classes?' ('Where do you fit in consumer classes?', Gardner, *The Sunday Times* 14 May, 2000). The detail and complexity of knowledge will allow advertisers to personalise adverts on websites and digital television. Apparently every person on average hits eight 'touch points' per day from which data can be analysed to look at them as a consumer. For financial services the most profitable to target are **clever capitalists**. All of these names suggest a group into which a target market may fall. So if you are not a clever capitalist are you a **dinkie** – dual income and no kids – or a **swell** – single woman earning lots of loot? You can find more of these on www.mediaknowall.com (see Resources).

Age is an important factor. The ASA's own research on the public's view on advertising in 2002 used the following categories:

- teenagers 16/17/18 year olds still at school;
- singles aged 20–24;
- parents with at least one child aged 5–14;
- empty nesters aged 50–60;
- the greys 65–75.

Audiences, Research and Targeting

Discuss

How do adverts attract our attention? Catchphrases, slogans and jingles are one way to remember. Why do you think you remember particular ones?

The age categories often used by agencies are: 0–15, 15–24, 24–35, 35–55, 55+. One company, CACI, even suggests that inferences can be made about people's ages from their first names.

Other factors the ASA research took into account were demographic factors such as regions (North versus South), urban versus suburban or small town and socio-economic segmentation. People may fall into more than one group and will change groups over time but one factor will be constant and that is gender. As most domestic consumer products are bought by women, they are a marketing group by definition of gender. But of course there are lifestyle differences within this group. So a woman might at one time be a housewife interested in buying food and household goods, a **yummie** – young urban mother; she might also be a full time worker interested in her career and her car and computer, a **swell**; also a mother caring for her family and providing holidays; but also deep down she is a woman desiring to be the star image on the silver screen and have hair to match. Each of these will be given different priorities in her life depending on whether she is pre-family, young family, leisured, affluent and middle-aged, or a retired **grey panther**, a senior citizen with opinions. In addition a woman might be categorised by her partner's social group if the socio-economic scale is used. This would not identify her personal needs and desires. She might, for example be a Reformer in attitude, but placed into group C by income.

So one can see how complex and difficult targeting is and therefore how important market research is for advertisers. Other categories have also existed. In the USA Values Attitudes and Lifestyles (VALS) was a psychographics list developed in the 1970s and similar to Young and Rubicam that included:

- Belongers: cautious, nest builders, stay at home – susceptible to pensions plans, insurance, DIY.

- Emulators: young, identity seekers, lacking self-confidence; susceptible to offers of group's acceptance and friendship.

- Emulator–Achievers: materialists, yuppies, acquisitive, attracted by consumer goods as sign of success.

- Societially–conscious Achievers: 'greying hippies' concerned with personal rather then professional fulfilment against conspicuous consumption, the 'green market'.

- Need Directed: minimum wage earner, they survive rather than consume and are not advertised at.

The postcode is still one of the most significant ways of segmenting the market. Experian, a global information firm developed a list of 19 types of consumers based only on addresses. In terms of geo-demographics the most well-known system is ACORN. This divides the consumer by types of house and is useful for postal advertising by postal code. Obviously this is not so useful for terrestrial television advertising, but it becomes important if we consider cable television as one of the ways in which consumers may become more accessible to television advertisers in the future with the new digital services and convergence.

3.5 Targets to sales

Once the target has been defined the trick is to catch their attention. Advertisers have to raise our awareness of the product. Our interest is aroused by targeting us as a specific market, and our desire is aroused for the product or service by an appeal to our innermost needs. This of course has to be translated into sales. Research has indicated that advertising is closely linked with the 'uses and gratification' model of the media which suggests that people use advertisements to gratify needs rather than the reverse. That is people are perhaps less manipulated and more active in their relationship with advertising than the passive hypodermic model would suggest (see Glossary under **media effects**). As a result the advertisers have to work carefully to create the need.

'[Advertisers] need understanding of the consumer's relationships with the product – how the target consumer thinks and feels about the product and how it is used and the way it fits in with their lives. It is wrong to begin thinking about the brand and its attributes and how to compete with rivals without first thinking of basic consumer requirements and habits and basic thoughts and beliefs' (Ogilvy, Benson and Mather, 1978). Attention to the needs of the audience informs not only the advertisement but also the packaging and where the product is positioned and distributed in the market place. The advertiser is asking, what will people buy?

In a rapidly changing world the 'needs' also change. This is therefore part of a highly co-ordinated marketing strategy that includes branding, slogans and jingles.

'Tense, nervous headaches?'

What the agency designs have to do though is not just raise our awareness of a campaign but also design the advertisement so that their intention is attached to a preferred reading by the audience. (Part 2 shows how this works by using connotative associations. Part 4 discusses how these preferred readings convey stereotypes and ideologies.) There may of course be **polysemic** readings of the images that may be intentional. The ambiguity and complexity of an image which can be read at several levels or in alternative ways may make the advertisement even more memorable than one where the message is clear and unambiguous. However, it is also possible for advertisements to be read in alternative ways by **consumers**. If the audience reads only part or changes the reading they can negotiate a different understanding or even an oppositional reading. This can in fact lead to a campaign having the opposite effect of that intended. It can alienate consumers. It was certainly true that advertisements intended to be funny but portraying women as irrational and pathetic did not have a good reception in the eighties and nineties particularly from feminist groups. For example, one series of advertisements had a woman driver stuck in her car waiting for the 'fourth emergency service' – the AA – to help her. Many felt that this advertisement stereotyped women as victims as well as seeming to make them appear to be incapable of action in a crisis.

3.6 Conclusion and a caveat

Although we can generally look at an advertisement and generalise about its target audience we must also be aware that there are certain limiting factors. These are the advertising codes that limit the use of certain images and language. These codes produced by the ASA for print and by the ITC (now Ofcom) for television broadcasting have an effect upon the advertisements themselves and therefore on their reading. For example, alcohol advertisements have strict rules that the actors who feature have to appear 25 years

of age or older. But a reading of such an advertisement which suggested the drink was *only* targeted at the over-25s because of the age of the characters would be inaccurate in the context of the whole marketing campaign, as it may well be targeting the 18–25 year range. It is therefore essential when designing or reading an advertisement that you check with the relevant codes for the guidelines that the professionals have to follow.

Advertisements are highly complex texts. Their aim is to sell a product to a target audience. In order to do this they use sophisticated techniques. Remember to always ask yourself some basic questions:

- Who is the target audience?

- Who is the ad talking to?

- Who is talking?

- Why have the particular images and ideas been used to target?

- What is the line of appeal?

- How has the advert picked up on intertextual and cultural knowledge to appeal?

In order to find out more about television audiences you can look at the BARB organisation which researches audience figures for television and assesses the audience appreciation.

Much information on advertising can be gained from the Advertising Standards Authority. In 2002 the ASA did research on people's attitudes to advertising, what it is and its role in society. Here are some of the things that people said about advertising quoted in their report:

- 'I think it's a necessary thing. It's good for information and if it's too much in your face then you tend to switch off.'

- 'You're in business, you've got to advertise.'

- 'Local football teams are sponsored by local businesses...we'd struggle without that.'

- 'Without advertising ITV wouldn't be there.'

- 'It's all round advertising, you are completely blitzed by advertising, it doesn't matter what you do, you tend to find a big advert.'

What do you think? Is advertising helping the commercial world and supporting society or does it develop ideas and needs which influence our behaviour? N.B. Remember the source of these quotes when discussing them.

Activities

Task Advertising and Television – a Partnership?

Use a stopwatch and time the number of minutes of advertising in one hour. You can do this quickly by recording one hour and then fast forwarding. Try this across terrestrial, satellite and cable companies if possible. Do this in peak time and choose to time before a junction point, for example from 6.50 p.m. to 7.50 p.m.

- How much time is given over to advertisements in that hour?

- How many advertisements appear in that hour?

- Is it different across channels?

- Use these recordings to analyse the target audiences and the types of programming around which they appear to show the link between the two.

Task Psychographics Campaign

Using ONE of the emotional appeals:

1. Design an advertisement campaign for a product such as toothpaste, deodorant, car, trainers, breakfast cereal, etc.

2. Write it down as a short narrative.

3. Show this to a partner to test that the narrative works and do any necessary editing for clarity.

4. Write a paragraph under the narrative explaining how it uses the line of appeal and who is the target audience .

Extension Task

Draw a storyboard of the advert. There are various versions of storyboards but for this one draw three columns. The first for the image frame, the second for the soundtrack (dialogue, music, sound effects) and the third to explain how each of the frames contributes to the line of appeal and targets the audience (use between 10 and 20 frames).

Brand Appeal has 'Man Appeal' (OXO ads)

Task 1. Choose one product with different brands such as tea, washing powder, cars, etc.

2. Record the advertisements.

3. Analyse each advert. Use a chart like the one below to make comparisons:

Image	Soundtrack	Comments

4. Conclude what the line of appeal might be and who you think was the target audience.

5. Compare the advertisements for each of the different brands.

6. How did the brands differentiate themselves?

Activities

Task Old vs. New

- Look at advertisements from an earlier period. Possible sources might be TV programmes such as *Washes Whiter*, old off-air recordings will also contain some gems and display advertisements could also be used from old magazines. Museums often sell postcards of old advertisements. Today old adverts can appear on greeting cards and there are several books on advertising that have images of old campaigns, such as Guinness.

- Having chosen your product and image, list how the campaign appears different or similar to a contemporary example for the same or similar product. Consider the representation of people, the settings, the language used, the claims made, and so on.

- Using an old advertisement as a starting point (this could be a postcard reproduction for example), create a new television campaign for the product.

- Decide on the target market; the line of appeal, the style of camera and editing; the soundtrack.

- Choose the narrative form of the advert, such as the **moral tale** or the **slice of life**.

- Write these down in a short proposal for the manufacturer of the product you are advertising.

- Additional activity – Draw the storyboard for your new advert.

Task Look at the list below developed by advertising agency Young and Rubicam. Think about friends and family. Can you put them into one of the four groups – Mainstreamers; Aspirers; Succeeders; Reformers?

1. **Mainstreamers**, who make up 40% of the population, and who like security, and belonging to a group.

2. **Aspirers**, who want status and the esteem of others. They like status symbols such as designer labels and expensive watches, and they live off credit and cash.

3. **Succeeders**, people who have already got status and control.

4. **Reformers**, who define themselves by their self-esteem and self-fulfilment.

• Do you think that this is a good way to divide up the market?

• What current advertisements on television would appeal to each of these groups?

Names and Ages

Task Using the age brackets of

under 15, 15–24, 24–35, 35–55, 55+:

• What first names would you put in each of the age categories?

• Where would you put the following names: Alfred, Rose, Eric, Anna, Ellen, Darren, Jane, Peter, Gary, Matthew, Harry, Kayleigh, Lisa, Charlotte and George?

• Can you suggest why ages are used?

• Do you think you would change these age groups radically or not?

Activities

Lifestyles

1. Study the list of lifestyles below:

Lifestyle Type	Types of needs	Types of products
Admiration seekers		
Pleasure seekers		
Security and stability seekers		
Anti-authority rebels		
Joiners –		
(wishing to be accepted, but not lead)		
Generation X –		
(don't know what they want and don't care)		
Materialists		
Complainers		
Do-gooders		
Survivors		
Achievers		
Experimentalists		
Working-class puritans		

2. Suggest the characteristics of each lifestyle and the types of products they would buy.

3. Choose one lifestyle and draw up the marketing proposal for an advertisement for a product that would appeal to that lifestyle. For example, Security and stability seekers could be attracted to a campaign for an insurance company that was selling security through pensions and house insurance products, but how would the idea of security translate into the images in an advert? One famous advertisement used this idea by showing several people opening inefficient umbrellas as it rained and the wind blew. The one exception was the umbrella supplied by the insurance company, the Legal and General, that opened without any problems or any holes and therefore provided security and protection for the consumer.

4.1 Advertising and Ideology

'Advertisements are selling us something besides consumer goods; in providing us with a structure in which we, and those goods are interchangeable, they are selling us ourselves.' (Williamson, 1978, p.13)

Adverts are selling us our insecurities and longings. This means that advertisements do not only sell commodities, they also create a 'structure of meaning' through a series of discourses and have an **ideological** function. They help to construct our beliefs about the world in the images they use, and in so doing they provide one route to **hegemony** over those views. They imply a norm and then tell us how to get it.

'Vorsprung Durch Technik': Audi

What does the Audi slogan suggest about the car? What are the meanings embedded in the slogan? I think it implies German efficiency and technology as superior. It sells us these beliefs through our desire to have the latest and best technology. Ownership of the car fulfils this.

Advertising and representation

Advertising re-presents the world to us. In this process certain ideas become representative for a whole group, or institution, or nation or place. The repetition fixes this image into a simplified formula or **stereotype**. These stereotypes can create beliefs (ideologies); for example the belief that women need make-up to appear attractive but that men wearing make-up is sexually dubious.

It is easy to criticise advertisements for their use of stereotypes such as the good housewife or the macho male. In fact adverts are often quite conservative and follow rather than create beliefs. But the use of these beliefs may have more serious effect than the question of make-up. Have a look at the mythic claims about beauty, age and creams in adverts. Recently in TV advertisements there have appeared some miraculous anti-ageing creams for women. Men obviously don't need them! At a certain level we can look at these advertisements and their world and know

that this is not reality – 'it's only an ad'. But this does not acknowledge the complex interaction between self-image and the advertisements. Even if we are not the target audience we are still being given messages. What are these messages? To take the example of the anti-ageing creams, there is the message of women having to work at staying young or at least having the appearance of youth. For women age is a stigma. There are other messages around these ads. The only ones that I have seen have been fronted by famous female white faces. I have yet to see one done by a famous black face.

> Why not? Perhaps black skin doesn't age? I don't think so – so there must be another reason. Can you think of one? Why are there no television advertisements for anti-wrinkle cream for ageing men?

In effect, even if we are not the target audience, we are being given messages about age, race and gender: about youth and age, about black and white faces, male and female faces and their importance and acceptability for this product. This is created through an illusion of **realism** as we read the advert – the text.

Advertising and readers

In Media Studies we talk about 'reading a text' and this perhaps needs a little more explanation. Every TV advertisement is carefully researched and tested before it is finally broadcast. There will be **qualitative** and **quantitative** research as well as psychographic research on the target audience. All of this research will be aimed at ensuring that the target audience gets the message; that is, they 'read' the advertisement in the way the advertisers want them to, i.e. the *preferred reading*. Many will read the advert in the preferred way, but others will read it with some provisions depending upon their age, race, experience, and so on. They will have a negotiated reading, but still may fall into the peripheral target area for the advertisers. Still others who are usually not the target audience will read the advert in an oppositional way challenging many of the claims it might make or finding the advert offensive in some way.

The activity sheet on page 56 should help you to realise that in order to understand how messages are constructed and to discover the discourses (as Foucault would have it) around these we need to see how a view of society or a version of reality is

Messages and Meanings

constructed in the media. The framework for analysing texts in Part 2, 'Decoding Advertisements', is one that will give you the evidence to critically evaluate any claim for a particular group of advertisements. The semiotic theory used there suggests that advertisements are not just indices of a product's worth, waiting to be 'read' where the message is overt, but a cultural construct with ideological effect. The effect is a result of the network of ideas and references within the discourse and this sets it into its social context. This includes the economic, legal, technological, as well as the production and consumption or 'reading' of the text.

Advertising and production

The production of a commodity is rarely signified in an advert. Occasionally it might be referred to in terms of heritage, such as the making of beer or spirits (e.g. Jack Daniels bourbon) or of bread, but we rarely see the contemporary factory. Such references to old-fashioned trades create a belief about the craftsperson working to give us these 'old-fashioned' values. Organisations such as Fair Trade and publications such as the *New Internationalist* have campaigned to bring the issue of production to the fore. Certain products that are either grown or produced in Third World and poor countries have been criticised for allowing their advertising campaigns to hide the means of production. Investigating products such as bananas, coffee, chocolate and trainers will reveal the differences between producers and consumers and expose the real cost of the products.

Advertising currency

Advertisements provide us with the 'exchange-value'. For example the campaign for diamonds – 'a diamond is

forever' – quoted in Williamson (1978) suggests that it is the diamond gift that generates love and therefore **metonymically** 'stands for' love. People and objects are interchangeable. The value, such as love, attaches itself to the product. It is the connection between the product and an abstract idea such as love that creates a belief that giving a diamond signifies love. Of course it does not. It signifies the message of the diamond company to buy its product.

In advertising, the product and object are often positioned next to each other. This is particularly so in perfume/aftershave adverts which appear most frequently in the pre-Christmas period. The purpose of this juxtaposition is confirmed by the model(s) taking on the shape and colour of the perfume/aftershave bottle. The consumer will then (hopefully) buy the aestheticised product in order to buy the image.

An advertisement does not only create a meaning. As part of a discourse it uses representations and meanings that are already part of society. An advertisement will use images, concepts and myths that have cultural specificity and understanding or ideology. It can take these structures and signifiers and re-use them to identify the beliefs with the product. So in our diamond example the reason that it works is that one of the beliefs in our society is that the only way to meet your ideal partner is through romance. The diamond in the advertisement signifies not just love but romantic love …eyes across a crowded room. There are of course other ways to meet a partner, such as dating agencies or arranged marriages, but these are not signified in the advertisement. The ideology presented (its exchange-value) by the advertisement and its linguistic anchorage is

NOTES:

that a diamond will guarantee romantic love – forever. Romantic love is one of the messages also used as currency by Mills and Boon romantic novels and Hollywood's romantic genre films such as *Pretty Woman* (1990). These texts have a mainly female audience. The diamond advertisement often has a male and female figure as signifiers, but which of them do you think is the target audience for the diamond advertisement?

stereotype thus gains its credence by being repeated as well as by its intertextuality.

Some stereotyping can be very powerful and have social consequences. Those stereotypes associated with race or disability for example can lead to much misunderstanding, whilst the image of thin young women has been of concern for its influence on eating disorders in women.

4.2 Stereotyping

Most of us use stereotypes and categorise people when we first meet them by their dress and non verbal communication. But it is when stereotypes are used to negatively categorise and the message is repeated so that a group is treated differently that this becomes a concern. Advertisements have to get their message across in a very short space of time. They therefore use stereotypes to convey, through a rapid shorthand, certain ideas about places and people. As you analyse more advertisements you will see how this works.

Stereotyping is a process by which one group categorises and describes another group. It is usually done by taking certain elements from the group that then stand for that group as a whole. So we could categorise a Frenchman by saying that he would wear a striped jersey, have a moustache, carry onions, ride a bike, be a romantic lover and so on. We know that the number of Frenchmen who match this stereotype is insignificant, even if they exist at all. This image is one that achieves its mythic status by repetition.

Other stereotypes such as the white coated and bespectacled scientist are also used as a shorthand for being the expert or having the knowledge. This use of signifiers appears in other media forms such as comics and films. In *Spellbound* (1945) for example, Ingrid Bergman who plays a psychiatrist is seen at the beginning dressed in a white coat, wearing severe glasses and with her hair tightly bound. By the end of the film, as she becomes the romantic heroine rather than the psychiatrist, all of these iconic symbols have disappeared. This use of glasses to signify 'geek' and white coat to indicate science are still used regularly throughout the media. The

4.3 Gender, stereotyping and ideology

Gender is a significant area of stereotyping. 'Boys don't cry' is a phrase that you may have heard when you were a child. What effect does that phrase have on you today when you see a man cry? One famous very public occasion when a sporting idol was seen to cry was the footballer Paul Gascoigne, 'Gazza', during the 1990 World Cup competition. This incident led to many references to it in the media, such as *Spitting Image* and in a Walkers crisp advert with Gary Lineker, mainly for comic purposes. What effect would this repetition of the event have on men and their attitude to showing their emotions? In other cultures it is quite acceptable for men to show their distress and cry. What do you feel about these nationalities when you see such behaviour? Is there a small part of you that thinks they are not 'real' men?

This is how stereotyping can influence the way we think about other cultures and how what appears to be a natural belief or truth is in fact a very complex process of construction. How are men referenced in advertisements? There are certain stereotypes such as Jack the lad, the Romeo, the lager lout, the boss, the weakling, the macho, the family man, the hen-pecked husband, the jock, the caring 'new' man. The images that dominate tell us much about society.

Stereotypes do change. This is because they are related to power relationships. When a new group becomes more powerful their control over their representation may influence others. The position of women in society has changed over the last 50 years.

Messages and Meanings

The post-war 'little woman' in the house fulfilling her housewife duties whilst wearing her apron and sending her husband and children off into the world, was superseded in the eighties with the feisty, dominant image of the business woman power dressed with her shoulder pads and apparently in control. This was seen in such advertisements where women turned bowls of food onto men's heads or metaphorically castrate them by cutting their ties, or threw their rings and fur coats away but kept the car keys. In pop music, Madonna and later the Spice Girls helped to construct and reflect this new more overtly aggressive sexuality that was seen in advertisements.

But adverts were still in the main conservative. In the seventies and eighties research had shown that 56 per cent of representation of women in TV advertising portrayed them as housewife-mother role (Dominick and Rauch 1971). This research also found that:

- 71 per cent of women were aged apparently in the 20–35 bracket;

- the majority of these women were being used to sell products to men where their presence was irrelevant to the product.

Other research (Goffman 1972) discovered that:

- women were often positioned lower than men;

- they were often featured as being sexually available, e.g. with their legs apart or arms held up over their heads lying down or across over something such as a sofa;

- they were rarely shown as being serious – rather, smiling and laughing, being child-like;

- they were frequently shown caressing their bodies.

If you did the same piece of research today would the results be similar or different? As we have said much of this representation is linked to the concept of power in society. To have power over something/someone by looking at them is said to be **voyeuristic**. This has often been associated with the male gaze or 'look' over women (Mulvey 1975; Goffman 1972; Dyer 2002). It can of course refer to other power relationships such as the power of a Western viewer over the image of a starving child from the Third World.

Another message seen in many advertisements is of a women waiting for her 'prince' to come, constructing a rather passive role for women. John Berger (1972) said, 'Men act and women appear. Men look at women. Women watch themselves being looked at...This determines not only relations between men and women but also the relation of women to themselves...Thus she turns herself into an object and most particularly, an object of vision.'

One way to explore this is to look at how sports women are used in adverts in comparison with men. Theirs is an active role and building strength and muscle is required. How are they photographed and used? Is there a difference? 'To be both female and strong today violates traditional roles of feminine identity...' (Balsamo 1996). If you compare the way female sports bodies are used in adverts with fashion ads or in male-orientated magazines there is a remarkable similarity. Could this be said about male sports people? Look at the adverts around the Olympics or other sporting events where there are women competitors such as Wimbledon.

NOTES:

4.4 Women, roles, class and image

Female representation in advertisements has been traditionally situated in two areas: the Madonna and the Magdalene. This is a binary opposition between the domestic woman and the sexually active whore. In the fifties as a result of the movement to get women back into the domestic environment from their roles in factories, farms and the services after the War, the mother and wife was the emphasis. The focus was on domestic consumption: 'We helped them to rediscover that home-making is more creative than to compete with men...' (Ernest Dichter, Psychologist in Advertising in *Washes Whiter*). The wife or mother provided the service for the husband and children. The Madonna was the key image. As sexual liberation took hold in the sixties, partly as a result of the contraceptive pill, women were provided with the fantasy of economic freedom as well as sexual freedom. The emblems of these were the glamorous – rather than mummsy images on the screen, the Magdalene image dominated. But even so as Barthes commented in his deconstruction of the Omo advertisement, dirt was a 'diminutive enemy' and the woman was the liberator in the fight against this enemy. (Barthes, 'Soap Powders and Detergents', in *Mythologies*, 1972).

'You'll look a little lovelier each day with wonderful pink Camay'

What other lines of appeal were there which created beliefs about society? Fantasy and aspiration dominated in the bleak post-war period in the fifties. Starlets appeared dressed as goddesses and using products that enhanced their ethereal beauty. Women luxuriated in baths. Remember many houses did not have bathrooms and if they did they were so cold you jumped in and out of the bath very quickly; but when you bought the bar of soap you also bought the fantasy of the bath experience you saw on the screen. This was its exchange-value.

The Hollywood image of the dumb blonde in films such as *Gentlemen Prefer Blondes* (1953) was to have consequences for the role models that appeared in advertisements. If you were appealing to men, blonde was good; but for advertising to women, brunettes were used, especially when the product was aspirational. Class was still very much in evidence and the stereotypes associated with them. The great unwashed suffered from BO and the role of the product was to help you not only get romance but also get a job and raise your class status. Very often job promotion happened after you had used deodorant.

The sixties on the other hand was a decade where being of a lower class became something to celebrate. The Beatles and other pop icons kept their regional accents and working-class images, as did many successful actors, such as Albert Finney. Success was therefore an achievable status for many young people. It seemed that it didn't matter where you came from you could still achieve success and fame and advertisements played upon this belief.

'Fry's Turkish Delight – Full of Eastern Promise'

The relaxation of sexual mores with the advent of the contraceptive pill meant that advertisements could refer to sexual satisfaction more explicitly. Often food adverts used this with the mouth substituting for sexual erogenous zones. This freedom allowed men to play on the fantasy of availability of sex. 'Jack the lad' appeared in advertisements, picking up on images seen in the media such as the *Carry on...* films, and the Benny Hill shows. There were confused messages about gender roles with feminists being critical of language and images while men could see women of apparently easy virtue on the screen. Women on the other-hand wanted more equality with their new sexual liberation. A lipstick could reference a belief in sexual excitement and be a male fantasy in which a woman was objectified. But did women acquiesce in this fantasy or did they read it differently as being assertive?

Women's roles were becoming more powerful in society but this reality was not always reflected in the advertisements. Even businesswomen were seen out of the office rather than in it. Why did advertisers maintain these rather old-fashioned stereotypes? Research showed that women preferred to see a man in charge even where the message was one of independence. It was not feminine to be seen as the boss. The relationship between men and women and their roles in society were changing more slowly than the 'chattering classes' believed. For example, whereas men could be seen

Discuss
Do you believe that Berger's 1970s comment 'men act, women appear' is still the case in contemporary advertising?

Messages and Meanings

as all pals together in the pub, at the club or at the game, women seemed still to reference themselves by the men in their lives and their domestic environment. Getting your 'prince' was still the ideological norm for most women.

Plus ça change

Advertising agencies need to know their market and then as now much time was spent on analysing the gender perspective, sometimes unsuccessfully. Most of the people working in the industry were male and the majority of the creative teams were male so when Big Green Door, a market research company looked at women's responses to advertisements (Brinkworth, *The Sunday Times*, 28 November,1993) the results were unsurprising. Adverts that were for household products were seen as 'typical,' 'patronising', while women's inner selves were 'caring, sexy, ambitious, daring and independent'. But this did not translate into new gender roles in adverts. Women found the macho man appealing, but the image of the new man in the kitchen did not work; 'it doesn't ring true' was a general comment. So in reality the domestic roles were still quite fixed while women's own inner desires were not reflected in these domestic roles.

'The Nineties woman is more assertive, capable and self-assured. She has sex appeal but doesn't flaunt it so obviously' (quote from a model agency *The Sunday Times*, ibid.).

But does research support this view? In the 1990s Guy Cumberbatch, a media researcher, analysed how advertisements portrayed the sexes in research for the Broadcasting Standards Council. The results showed:

• half of the females shown looked between 21 and 35 compared with only 30 per cent of men;

• over half the men portrayed looked over 30;

• at peak viewing times women were depicted either in the domestic environment or as attractive ornaments;

• in 85 per cent of cases authoritative figures, such as bank managers and teachers, were portrayed by men;

• nine out of ten used a male voice-over to narrate.

In advertisements aimed at women feminists claim that there has been a tendency to identify women with the commodity. So there are often phrases such as 'you and …make a great team'. The packet/bottle/box helped the woman not to fail in whatever domestic task was set in front of her. The line of appeal was clearly to inadequacy. This then translated into the real world where the woman would have to be helped to achieve results. If you study Hollywood films for example you can see this repeated as in *Pretty Woman, Dirty Dancing* (1987) and *Save the Last Dance* (2001). Feminists would here indicate that in a patriarchal hierarchical society this idea helps to maintain the ideological belief of women as subservient.

Gender roles are not specific to adults. A review of research into this area was carried out in 1995 looking at the way children perceived gender roles in television commercials. The results of the studies showed amongst other things that boys tended to reject any female role models for example using toys, whereas girls were happy to use ones where the role model was male, although were more favourable to female role models. In fact some research showed that girls between 7–11 actually responded more favourably to male than female role models (Griffiths, et al 1995).

NOTES:

4.5 The family

The family is one of the strongest signifiers in Western society. The structure might have changed significantly but we still have a belief about the worth of the family. Women are frequently targeted through their children. Their success is judged by the quality of their children's diet, clothes, health, the cleanliness of the house, and so on. The most important relationship is between mother and daughter. The mother is teaching the daughter the best products to use to be a good housewife.

The seventies and eighties was a period in which feminism carved out new roles for women resulting in confusing messages. The mother often played the role of provider but the corollary to this was that the children were vulnerable because the mother was at work. Katy in the OXO advertisements was an example. For many years Katy spent her life in the OXO ads serving up meals for her husband and friends. But in the nineties Katy had a life outside the kitchen and was so organised and such a superwoman that she made the meal in advance. Katy rushed home from her classes/work only to find the meal finished by her famished family leaving none for her. The overt message was that the meal was so good (because of OXO) that the family couldn't wait. But was there a sub-text? Was Katy being punished for not being there to put it on the table? Her plate was empty!

The family profile in the twenty-first century has changed since the eighties. How have advertisers responded? For many years the ideology of the family has been something that has underpinned many advertisements. Now one-parent families, as a result of divorce and lower marriage rates, may mean that to show mother, father and children as the ideal would alienate many people who might be the target audience. Has this resulted in less use of the family, parents and children as an iconic image?

The use of gender and sexual references were also changing. The eighties had seen a new social-economic environment. The Thatcherite era saw an ideology of individualism and more equal opportunity legislation. The image of powerful women led to the corollary of apparently less powerful men. AIDS was beginning to be addressed as a major global issue and overt sexual innuendoes were seen as irresponsible. How were the advertising agencies going to address the new social climate? Sex sells so what would replace it as a selling tool?

4.6 The not so naughty nineties

The ninties saw a significant move to advertising strategies that suggested less materialistic values. The environmental message was strong. Companies tried to sell us the idea that they were ecologically caring and socially responsible. Nostalgia played an important part, going back to a mythical past (Mrs Thatcher famously talked about Victorian family values). And for men there was the chance to be reinvented and become a 'new man'. It was OK to look after your children for the day – but you would never be quite as good as your multi-tasking partner at it, because this was still not really man's work. You could change a nappy – just. You could go in the kitchen and cook. You were thoughtful and your feminine side was evident.

In the nineties the advertisers experimented with this type of role-reversal. But in fact it still did not reflect the reality of many people's lives. Research showed that women still did the majority of domestic chores. The trend in the nineties was said to be a 'neo-traditionalism'. What this phrase meant after the turmoil of 'the sexual revolution' was that men and women returned to their traditional roles but not quite with the same stereotypes as before. Women, for example, could be seen to own and drive the (small) car for example. There was also a trend to more exotic and romantic imagery replacing the overt sex images. The Nicole/Papa adverts for the Renault Clio are an example of this.

4.7 Men in advertising

The role of men, like that of women, has changed significantly since the 1950s when television advertising first started. The fifties was still a patriarchal society with men having the more dominant roles. Professional women who worked were usually unmarried. Once married, most

Messages and Meanings

women stopped work and certainly so after having a child. In fact there were some occupations where it was a requirement that a woman stopped work on marriage. Often women did the same job for less pay. For working-class women work was always necessary but it tended to be shift work, part-time and low paid to fit in with the family. Often therefore it was the man who had control of the money being spent in a household. Any major purchase whether it was a washing machine, a cooker, a vacuum cleaner or a car had to get male approval. This was partly why advertisers used men in so many adverts for an apparently female target audience.

How were men represented in these adverts in the early decades? They were mainly dressed in suits; they were at work; or they were there to tell women what was the best buy. Very often a man would appear at the end of the advert to deliver the final lecture on how to get clean washing, or make a meal. If they didn't actually appear they were present in the male voice-over delivering the message.

But how were adverts aimed at men constructed? Men were often seen in the company of other men, perhaps at the pub, club or at some sporting event. They were also clean-shaven, clean cut, formally dressed. They were rarely seen as part of the domestic environment. Changes occurred over the subsequent decades. The sixties saw the James Bond suave and sophisticated image become popular, followed in the seventies by the image of the 'free spirit', the independent man. The eighties was a period of Jack the lad, the stereotype of the Essex man who made his wealth and spent it on luxuries. The nineties was the period of the 'new man' a reconstructed male who would be comfortable looking after children and

being seen to do some domestic chores, a caring man.

The New Man? Eternity, from Calvin Klein

Do you think this image would sell today? What image has the new millennium brought? Is the man still clean-shaven and formally dressed? What roles do men play today in adverts?

4.8 Age – the generation gap

We have noted that many of adverts use attractive young adults to sell, but they also use children and older people. Often they are used in campaign adverts such as drink-driving where children and elderly people are seen to be the more vulnerable section of society. In Part 5 we will look at the rules governing advertising to children but

NOTES:

what roles do children play in adverts that are targeted at adults? Are they used to define adult roles? Do they reinforce gender as well as age stereotypes or not?

What are the roles given to older people in adverts? Does it depend upon the product and the target audience? Saga is a company that deals with products for the retired. Their advertising uses very active, healthy, seemingly wealthy and attractive older models. But there are many older people who have none of these attributes. Most advertisers would not consider old people as their target market because of their lack of spending power. But they will use older people to perhaps deliver a message such as 'the family'.

Some adverts have been criticised for their representation of older people as a target for the butt of a joke. What do you think? One advert that was criticised was for a magazine. In the advert the magazine is being avidly read by a meals-on-wheels deliverer in her van whilst an old person is seen sitting in the house waiting for the meal. The message was obvious – this magazine was so good that you would forget what you were doing, no matter how important. But what if you were an old person who relied on the delivery of a meal for their daily nourishment, would you think this was an appropriate reference? If you have an elderly relative, such as a grandparent who is in this position, would you think it was funny for them to have to wait?

There have also been concerns about the way that adverts may influence children's behaviour: 'Because children both observe and learn from the characters portrayed in advertisements, obvious potential exists for the shaping and reinforcement of gender stereotypes' (Courtney and Whipple 1983, in Hoek and Lawrence 1998). There has also been a suggestion that violence in adverts, as in other forms of media, could influence children's behaviour and perceptions. This is a complex area of study for further reading. Look at the work of researchers such as David Buckingham and others on children and media effects.

4.8 Race

The Heineken debacle over the sponsorship of *Hotel Babylon*, where a

manufacturer tried to get a programme altered because it had the 'wrong' mix of faces, raised issues of control of content through sponsorship (see Part 5) but also the issue of how multi international companies can advertise to local and national sensibilities. In Western countries we have tended to see black faces in advertising for sport products and fashion. In Britain there have been adverts that have shown people from ethnic minorities as 'ordinary' consumers rather than musicians, entertainers or sports people and this reflects the attempts of television companies to address the 'institutional' racism that is reflected in the choice of casting and programming. (This issue is explored in *Race in the Frame*, a video educational package produced by the BBC.) But the placing of black and other ethnic groups in ads has been an issue in advertising. It is rare that an advert uses black or Asian faces in an ordinary situation. This issue was also referenced in the Hoek and Lawrence article (1998) with regard to Maori faces in children's advertisements in New Zealand. The 'Brown Pound' is becoming a more important area for advertisers. It is said to be worth £32 billion according to a recent industry report (*The Observer*, 22 August 2004).

4.9 Conclusions

There are other possible areas of representation such as how institutions such as the police or education or hospitals are represented in adverts. Everyone holds beliefs that have been culturally constructed. For instance, it is a commonly held belief in our country that formal education is good. This belief has been challenged in totalitarian states because it has been seen as a way for the State to control society through educating young people's minds to one viewpoint. Your choice of adverts will identify the type of representations to study. But whatever the advert, there will be some form of representation and with it a message to the target audience.

Beliefs can change over time such as the ideal family and gender roles, but they are always very powerful. It is their apparent 'obviousness' that makes them so powerful. The role of the advertiser is to use these beliefs or ideologies, to help sell a product or a service. Advertising continues to deal in superficial clichés but brings with them deeper discourses.

Discuss
What current adverts use images of old people? What role do they play in the advert? What are the messages?

Discuss
Who might be offended by the slogan 'Everyone's a Fruit and Nut case' for a chocolate bar?

Activities

 **Products and Brands**

- Choose a product (not a brand) such as an anti-wrinkle cream, hair colour product or mobile telephones of which there are several brands being advertised.

- Divide into pairs with each pair taking a different brand in the product range to analyse their advertisement.

- Depending on the product you could use categories such as race, ethnicity, gender, disability and age to analyse their messages.

- You will need to analyse the adverts and the elements that make up each of them fairly carefully and in a structured form. Each group should have a similar set of criteria from which they are working.

- Having done a semiotic analysis, look at your results as a class/group. For each of the following questions your answers should refer directly to the advertisement you have analysed. You are trying to find out how the image constructed and what the image says about the product from the elements:

  1. What type of person is in the image?

  2. How are they dressed, how do they behave (NVC)?

  3. Do the adverts reflect the reality of the world you see everyday outside of the media world?

  4. Are there any groups missing in these advertisements? Can you suggest why?

  5. What view of society is suggested?

  6. Do you think these are true or false views?

  7. Who do you think is the target audience?

Extension Task

Now compare your results across the range of adverts with the other groups:

1. Can you come up with any general statements across all the brands?

2. Do these say anything about the way that the chosen product has constructed a particular view of the world (reality)? What do they suggest about the product and the type of people that the advertisers are targeting and by implication who does *not* inhabit that world?

Activities

Task **Representation of Gender – Men**

• Collect images from newspapers, magazines, advertisements of men playing different roles.

• Put them into similar groups such as the professional man; the caring man; the macho man; the sporting man; the family man; the lover, and so on. Stick them on large sheets of paper. Is there any significant dominant role in your collection? What overall image is given of masculinity?

This activity could be repeated with teenagers and children and with women.

Task **Representation of Gender – Women**

• Select roles you think might appear for adult women in advertisements, such as the sex kitten, the girlfriend, the mother, the wife, the mistress, the daughter, the witch, the bitch, the gossip, etc.

• Taking advertisements during a range of peak time viewing, how many times do these roles appear? (To do a more accurate comparison you would need to count how many times women appear in total.).

Women and Images

Task • If you have done the Representation of Women activity and collected images of women you could use these to test Goffman's idea on images of women. Use magazines as well as looking at a range of television advertisements.

• You could draw up a chart to collect statistical information using Goffman's list. Does your research support or challenge Goffman?

4.5.1 Representation of Families

 • Select two advertisements that represent different families. Analyse how these differences are constructed.

•Look at the members of the family and their apparent ages, the way they are dressed, etc., their activities together, their home or other location they are seen in, identify their class and racial group.

Draw up a chart using the following:

Elements	Family A	Family B
Soundtrack		
Technical codes		
Camera		
Lighting		
Editing		
Family group		
Location/home (mise-en-scène)		
Activities		
Class		
Race		
Intertextuality		

•What sort of audience do you think each advert targets?

•Why have each of the advertisers used a family as a signifier?

•What messages are being implicitly given about the family?

Activities

Men and Images

 Look at contemporary advertising images of men and apply the following questions to their analysis:

- What are the men doing?

- What is their facial expression – happy, serious...?

- What is their eye angle/direction? Why?

- Where are you, the viewer, positioned in relation to the man? Higher/lower?

- What objects are associated with the men?

- Where are they located?

- What parts of the body are naked or emphasised?

- Is there a woman with the man? What is her role?

- What is the product being sold?

- Consider your results and compare them with others. What conclusions do you come to about how men are represented?

Task Race and Ethnicity

- Using display adverts as well as television adverts, collect as many adverts as possible where there is a representation of an ethnic minority group as an ordinary consumer.

- List the products.

- Is there a range of different products or do some dominate?

- Is there any significance in the types of product that these adverts are selling and the target audience?

- Is there a range of different racial types such as Asian, Indian, Black? You could tabulate these to get accurate statistics and compare the products to racial types.

- Were these adverts relatively easy to find?

- Have a guesstimate as to the ratio of these adverts to the number of adverts you looked at.

Activities

Task Giving a Talk

1. Choose a category such as age, race, children, men, women, teenagers or an institution such as the nation.

2. Prepare a short talk. Your talk should cover such things as:

- the types of product and audiences targeted through representations of this group;

- the way the group is represented in general with some specific examples to illustrate your points;

- how this representation may have changed over time;

- any issues which you think the contemporary representation raises (such as anorexia for teenage girls).

The Advertising Industry and Its Regulatory Institutions

5.1 Background

Ever since advertising first appeared on television in Britain in 1955 it has been regulated. Why should this be so? Partly it is to do with a concern that advertisers do not claim things that the product cannot deliver; partly it is to ensure they do not breach the law; partly it is fear of the effects of advertising, particularly on the more vulnerable or gullible members of society. Originally the ITA (Independent Television Authority) was in charge, followed by the IBA (Independent Broadcasting Authority) that also regulated commercial radio; then in 1990 the ITC (Independent Television Commission) with its lighter regulatory touch took over (regulation for commercial radio was taken over by the Radio Authority) and since December 2003 Ofcom has been in charge of regulating broadcast advertisements.

The ITC had the statutory power from the 1990 Broadcasting Act to regulate television advertising up to the Communications Act 2003 and had a published Code of Advertising Standards and Practice. This code is now being used by Ofcom and will probably be used by the Advertising Standards Authority (ASA) if it takes over the role of regulator of broadcast advertising for radio and television under Ofcom. Because of the changing nature of this area it is advisable to check the current situation by looking on the websites of these organisations (see Resources).

In addition all advertising is subject to the Committee of Advertising Practice's Code, the CAP Code and the Code of the European Advertising Standards Alliance. You can check these out on the relevant websites. So there are a myriad of rules to negotiate for the advertising business, but for today's regulators there is an almost impossible task in controlling the new media. The multiple systems within global communications mean we are subject to many more messages than before and inevitably these include advertising for all sorts of commodities. You will probably have received spam on your home computer and personalised adverts on your mobile phone. Many of these are for services you would never want. The new interactive digital world creates the ability to tailor messages to individuals. This not only targets more efficiently, but also opens the possibility of buying directly and immediately.

> What do you feel about these newer forms of advertising? Are they an intrusion or a welcome source of information? How would you regulate this type of advertising? If we accept advertising interrupting other forms of entertainment should it be allowed in these newer media? We are in fact facing the same question that previous generations did but with different media.

5.2 Commercial television and advertising

'Schhh... you know who' (Schwepps)

The structure of commercial television has changed rapidly over the last few years. ITV started in 1955 as a group of regional broadcasters such as Granada and TVS who negotiated individual deals with advertisers but were regulated centrally by the ITA. By the nineties the rules of ownership had been relaxed and many of the regional television companies became part of much larger communication and publishing companies. In 2004 Granada and Carlton merged to form ITVplc in an attempt to retain control of terrestrial commercial television. (More detail on the history of Independent TV can be found in Part One.)

The expansion and convergence of the media is one of the reasons that the Government has introduced the new regulator Ofcom to try to cope with a 'mediascape' that is becoming more and more complex. Here we are concerned with television advertising, but remember that this is only part of a much wider global media economy.

In the United Kingdom the Advertising Code for Television has had three objectives:

- to ensure that television advertising is not misleading;

- to ensure that advertising does not encourage or condone harmful behaviour;

- to ensure that television advertising does not cause widespread or serious offence.

The Advertising Industry and Its Regulatory Institutions

Is it legal, decent, honest and truthful?

What has been the role of the regulators? Their functions have been to ensure that advertisers keep to the code, and are truthful, and to oversee the laws linked to advertising in respect to such things as smoking and alcohol, libel and the Trades Description Act. The licensees, who are the companies that have the licence to broadcast, must comply with the rules on scheduling and the number of adverts shown in a given period. They also have to follow rules such as the identification of adverts and programmes as separate units.

The current regulations for television advertising can be found on the Ofcom website (see Resources). At the time of writing (February 2004) they are using the codes laid down by the ITC. There is at present a proposal that this regulatory role will be passed to the Advertising Standards Authority (ASA Broadcasting) to oversee advertising in broadcasting, the cinema, as well as its present role in print (Cozens, *The Guardian*, 27 October 2003). In this discussion I am taking the website of February 2004 as the guidelines. You will need to check these later amendments.

The advertising industry has long been lobbying for a move towards greater self-regulation in television advertising, like the role played by the ASA for print publication and the PCC (the Press Complaints Commission) for newspapers. They claim that media convergence means a new regulatory system is required. The proposal is that the BACC (Broadcasting Advertising Clearance Centre), the organisation that checks storyboards and scripts and which is run by the broadcasters, would continue to vet adverts before they go on screen, but regulation would pass from the TV authority to a self-regulatory body.

Ofcom has been concerned with the structure of commercial television and has lifted the ban on Channel 4, Channel 5 and BSkyB selling their advertising air-time jointly, paving a way for the merger of their sales operations. This follows the merger of Carlton and Granada in February 2004 to form ITVplc. There will therefore in all likelihood be only two major advertising broadcasters from which to buy air-time for the advertisers instead of the many regional as well as national channels they negotiated with previously.

Who will not be pleased with this move? The advertisers will not and they have argued against such a consolidation because it would limit competition from broadcasters for their advertisements. They prefer the divide and conquer principal. ITV made £1.68bn from advertising in 2003 and 70 per cent of this was from special deals made with media buyers. The concern about the merger between Granada and Carlton therefore for advertisers is about such a large company (ITVplc) being able to abuse its dominant position in the market to negotiate even better deals with the media buyers. (To see where the media buyer's role appears in the making of an advertisement look at Part 3.4.) As a result it is proposed that an adjudicator be appointed to police any disputes, such as the rates charged for advertising on the networks, which arise between the merged ITV companies and advertisers.

NOTES:

5.3 Does the watchdog have teeth?

Both the ASA and the ITC have been called 'toothless' watchdogs of the advertising code. The ASA, for example, allowed the controversial Benetton advertisements through. One example of these was of a picture of a man dying of AIDS. One showed a water bird covered in oil, another a new-born baby complete with umbilical cord. These adverts were being used to sell colour co-ordinated jumpers and created much debate. (Further information on these campaigns can be found on the ASA website School and College section under regulation, and taste and decency; and other sites such as www.mediaknowall.com. There are also documentaries on the Benetton and other campaigns that can be accessed via the Video Studio, Richmond upon Thames - see Resources.)

Would these advertisements have been shown on television? Quite a few television advertisements are rejected at the planning stage. All storyboards and scripts have to be vetted before the advertisements are made and even then they can be rejected when seen. They are checked to see that they comply with the ITC (now Ofcom) code. One example of the effects of such vetting was of Levi 501 jeans in which the boy in the advert took off his jeans and put them in the laundrette machine with some stones. There were two concerns: firstly, that the sight of white Y-fronts might be offensive; secondly, that there might be copycat behaviour with stones liberally appearing in Britain's launderettes. The Y-front problem was solved by putting the boy in boxer shorts, and the stones were never an issue. Levi's jeans sales soared (as did those of boxer shorts).

Another product that raised controversy was for female sanitary wear. In particular an advert featuring Clare Rainer in which women discussed the advantages of a particular product was felt to be offensive because it was too 'in your face'. Although these products had begun to be promoted on television it was done by 'substitution' with women singing and dancing or enjoying similar activities which were then freeze-framed once the period started. The activity resumed once the product was used. The Claire Rainer adverts were withdrawn after complaints to the ITC that were concerned not only with the bluntness of the discussion, but also with the timing of the adverts. As a result sanitary adverts were banned between 4 p.m. and 9 p.m. and all day on school and public holidays.

Another advert that hit controversy was for a male deodorant in September 2003. This advertisement for Right Guard showed a man running down a dust-filled stairwell with an American accented reporter commenting on the progress of the 'game' to find out how effective the deodorant was. Can you think why this advertisement attracted complaints?

Most were about its similarity to images of the effects of the attack on the World Trade Centre. The company re-edited the advert to take out the stairwell scene and to more clearly signal that it was a game not reality. But even the re-edited version attracted complaints from viewers offended by the very idea that such a situation could be considered suitable material for a 'game' in the light of recent events. An even shorter version was eventually passed. This is an interesting case study to show how important context is. If this advertisement had been shown in 2000 there would probably have been no complaints about it. Other events such as war, child abuse, drugs, immigration and issues such as sexuality can influence people's sensibilities to adverts.

Heard it Through the Grapevine? Or watched it on the telly? Levi's 501 jeans relaunched in the 1980s.

If you were advertising an old-fashioned sweet and had in your storyboard a child being given a sweet by an old man, perhaps a grandparent, what current events or issues might be raised in the viewer's mind?

5.4 Children and advertising

'The Milky Bars are on me!'

In order to look at the issue of regulation in some depth we are going to focus on children and television advertising (there are other sections of the Ofcom code that could also be explored in detail).

A recent *Daily Telegraph* survey (August 2004) suggested that 49% of children watch more than four hours of television a day.

Here are some of the guidelines that Ofcom give for advertising to children. It follows the ITC guidelines:

- Advertising must not take advantage of children's inexperience or their natural credulity and sense of loyalty.

- Advertisements for products of interest to children must take into account the level of experience of those in the relevant age groups so as to avoid arousing unrealistic expectations.

- If advertisements for products of interest to children show or refer to characteristics which might influence a child's choice, those characteristics must be easy for children of the appropriate age to judge.

- Except in the case of television services carrying advertising directed exclusively at non-UK audiences, advertisements for expensive toys, games and comparable children's products must include an indication of their price.

- Where advertising for a children's product contains a price, the cost must not be minimised by the use of words such as 'only' or 'just'.

- Advertisements must not directly advise or ask children to buy or to ask their parents or others to make enquiries or purchases.

- Advertisements must not imply that children will be inferior to others, disloyal or will have let someone down, if they or their family do not use a particular product or service.

- Children in advertisements must not comment on product or service characteristics in which children their age would not usually be interested.

- Advertisements which offer to sell products or services by mail, telephone, email, Internet or other interactive electronic media must not be aimed at children.

- Advertisements must not contain material which could lead to social, moral or psychological harm to children.

- Advertisements must not contain material which could lead to physical harm to children.

The guidance notes list such activities and settings as: copying dangerous or antisocial behaviour, action that seems realistic rather than fantasy, live action rather than cartoon, behaviour and a hero who are seen as 'cool', road safety issues, dangerous domestic situations, medicines and chemicals, dangerous machinery, matches and fire, playing near water, digging caves in sand dunes, and other similar activities. It also lists the following:

- Bullying – advertisements must not encourage bullying.

- Vulnerability – advertisements must neither encourage children to go off alone or with strangers nor show them doing so.

- Sexuality – advertisements must not portray children in a sexually provocative manner.

NOTES:

- Distress – advertisements likely to cause distress to children must not be shown in children's programmes or in programmes likely to be seen by significant numbers of younger children.

- Use of scheduling restrictions – appropriate timing must be applied to advertisements which might harm or distress children of particular ages or which otherwise are unsuitable for them.

The ITC had an 'Ex Kids' restriction that excluded some advertising around children's programmes for under eights. As advertising broadcasting is unpredictable, unlike programming where parents can see the schedules, the following guidance was given for advertisers:

- Ex Kids restriction would avoid children up to 4 years old;

- post 9 p.m. will avoid most 5–8 year olds;

- later restriction (e.g. post 11 p.m.) will avoid most 9–12 year olds.

This might sound like quite a lot of regulations, but for some people it is still not enough. The proposed changes for a lighter, self-regulatory touch are being questioned by lobby groups and politicians. The MP Debra Shipley believes that self-regulation of television advertisements by the ASA would not be as effective as the previous ITC regulator, even if Ofcom takes on a supervisory role. She introduced a Bill into Parliament in 2003 'to prevent food and drink advertising during pre-school children's television programmes and related scheduling' (www.parliament.the-stationery-office.co.uk). It is proposed that Ofcom will take a research role in regulating advertising rather than handling individual complaints, so it will be the co-regulators who would look at scheduling of specific adverts, for example, while Ofcom would look at the more general questions such as the 9 p.m. **watershed**.

In November 2003 the power of the media over children was discussed in a study, called *Young People, Media and Personal Relationships* published by the BSC (Broadcasting Standards Commission) based on research with 9 to 17 year olds. The research found that young people were quite media literate and realised they are being manipulated. They also realised that sex was being used to sell. Interestingly in another study parents expressed real concern about the effects of so much sex being used in ads. So there is quite a distance from what children say to what parents believe about the influence of advertising. The Opium perfume advert in which Sophie Dahl appeared naked lying down with an arched back produced an interesting gender divide. The 10 year old boys were uncomfortable with it and said she was being exploited. Another gender factor was the link between an advert and homosexuality. The younger boys avoided any contact with this type of imagery, such as the Levi jeans with a naked male torso, in case they were 'tainted' by it. On the other hand, the sexual connotations of many adverts were not understood by younger viewers.

Pester power

There have been many studies on the effects of the media on children, who are believed to be the most vulnerable to media message. These usually take a theoretical position such as the hypodermic model or the uses and gratification model. They also look at the effects on young people through copycat behaviour, de-sensitisation and cultivation theories. Media literacy is also part of the equation: young children seem to find it particularly difficult to distinguish between a programme and an advert especially when the advert is creating a fictional world of toys and cartoons. Children's experience is limited and they will naturally ask for what they see, and if what they mostly see is on television then as research in the 1980s showed 95 per cent of children will ask for something they have seen advertised on television. Probably nearly the same number of parents will succumb at least once to this 'pester power' and advertisers are aware of this.

In the scale of all advertising on television this might not appear important, but the amount that children have to spend in pocket money adds up to around £1 billion a year and that does not include the money spent by family and friends on presents. On the other hand, some researchers believe that children become more media literate the greater the exposure to these forms. All of us are constantly being 'persuaded' to do things but we become selective as we develop our media knowledge and literacy. Andrew Colman, Reader in Psychology at Leicester University, said being exposed to advertising is a necessary evil rather like childhood inoculation for whooping cough: 'People are initially highly vulnerable to germs…but are inoculated through mild attacks over a long period of time' (*The Guardian*, 2 October, 1990). This links to the idea of the inoculation theory of the long term effects of the media.

Does this ideal of media literacy actually work in practice? The advertising agency Ogilvy & Mather who were in charge of the Barbie Doll account revealed that they aimed to encourage girls to own more than one doll by making the dolls' outfits obsolete, just as in the adult fashion market 'working on their desires to collect different outfits. Like the Jesuits, we say get them young, and you've got them for life' (Geoff Hamilton-Jones, from Ogilvy & Mather advertising agency). So are we media literates or media dunces?

> **Have you ever used pester power? Did it work? Were you happy with the product when you got it?**

5.5 Case Study – children and food

'A Mars a day helps you work rest and play'

One aspect of advertising to children is snack food. Groups such as the Food Commission are lobbying for tighter rules governing food advertising to children. In recent years there has been a general concern about the levels of obesity particularly in children. The World Health Organisation (WHO) launched a campaign in March 2003 attacking the food industry. It blamed the rising levels of obesity in children on television advertising of such products as soft drinks, as well as the more sedentary lifestyles of young children particularly in the Western world. The report claimed that 'Part of the consistent and strong relationships between television viewing and obesity in children may relate to the food advertising to which they are exposed'. They also noted that children were targeted because they would pester adults for the product. The food campaign group Sustain (an alliance of more than 100 groups concerned with food issues) found that in 2002, 95 per cent of food advertising during children's TV programming was for fatty, salty or sugary foods.

In America where obesity and its health related problems have been obvious for longer, the food and drink industry has been lobbying – with the support of the American Government – to prevent the WHO publishing its report about child obesity, so powerful is the economic clout of the food and related industries in the USA. (Boseley, 'WHO takes on the soft drinks industry', *The Guardian*, 3rd March 2003).

'Don't forget the fruit gums, MUM!'

In the United Kingdom we have also had a high profile campaign against sponsorship and advertising of fast food to children. It has thrown up some interesting anomalies. In April 2003 Cadbury's was helping to sponsor a Government fitness programme aimed at children through their *Get Active* campaign. But it was estimated that in order to collect enough tokens to get a volley ball, posts and nets for their school, children would have to eat 5,440 bars of chocolate (Carter, 'Eat now, play later', *The Guardian*, 30 April 2003). The Consumers Association, an independent watchdog, said that the Cadbury's *Get Active* scheme was

NOTES:

The Advertising Industry and Its Regulatory Institutions

'an irresponsible ploy to encourage unhealthy eating among kids' and Sheila McKechnie, the then head of the Consumers Association said 'this type of corporate exploitation of children has to stop'.

What are the advantages of such schemes as collecting tokens for educational equipment? Partly for the advertisers it will mean that they can circumnavigate any broadcast regulations. It also builds brand loyalty. How many people have shopped at a particular supermarket chain so that their children can take tokens into school to gain another computer? In America such brand loyalty can be very influential. A Coca-Cola sponsored day at a school led to the suspension of a student who turned up in a Pepsi shirt.

> **Does your school or college have sponsorship links with local firms? Do you believe sponsorship is ethical, necessary, harmful or helpful?**

How does the ITC combat this type of marketing and pester power? Famously, ex-England footballer Gary Lineker has been a long-standing part of Walkers crisps advertising. But does Lineker encourage children to buy the brand and therefore consume unhealthy fast food? The effect can be seen in a survey conducted recently by asking 15–16 year olds which snack came to mind first. The result was that 93 per cent named the Lineker-endorsed brand of crisps.

In some European countries there are much tougher regulatory regimes for advertising to children. In Sweden advertising to under 12 year olds is forbidden. In Greece toy advertising is banned on television, while Finland, France and the Netherlands all have legal restrictions on adverts directed at children. Debra Shipley, in her speech to Parliament (*Hansard*, Columns 530–1, 6 May 2003) called for a similar ban on food and drink during toddler TV scheduling. She listed health organisations that supported her Bill. She also quoted a spokesperson from the advertising industry that claimed that if the Bill was successful 'less children's television will be broadcast. That seems to me rather threatening and also undermines the claims of the television companies that children's TV is a form of public service broadcasting' (*Hansard*, Column 531, 6 May 2003).

> **Why should there be the chance of less children's television if advertising was curtailed?**

There are additional benefits to targeting children and 'tweenagers': it builds brand loyalty and the child who pesters for the Walkers crisps will be the adult who buys the Walkers crisps.

As a result of pressure from consumer organisations and evidence from America, the government's watchdog, the Food Standards Agency, commissioned research into the effects of television advertising on children. Its report, published in September 2003, established beyond reasonable doubt the link between the promotion of foods and children's eating behaviour. The agency said that the promotion of food to children was dominated by television advertising of pre-sugared cereals, soft drinks, confectionery, savoury snacks and fast food outlets. Companies selling the top 10 brands in 2002 spent £339 million on TV advertising. The agency said that it was considering health warnings on packets and restricting advertising if food manufacturers did not address the issue voluntarily. In November 2003, the advertising industry was summoned before a committee of MPs investigating child health. They rejected calls for a ban on fast food advertising claiming there was no evidence to make a link between child obesity and fast food ads. The senior executives from the advertising agencies responsible for Walkers crisps and McDonald's campaigns said that the advertising required to sustain a brand lead meant that other routes would be found if television advertising was banned. (Perhaps mobile phones?) Behavioural change such as eating, anti-smoking and road safety campaigns had to be long term rather than obligatory. The celebrity Walkers crisp adverts were defended as only taking market share as opposed to increasing the consumption of crisps overall. On the other hand it was argued that you could improve the advertising, and therefore sales, of *healthy* foods – for example the sales of bananas have apparently gone up considerably as a result of tennis players being seen to eat them.

> **Is there a contradiction here between what Walker's crisps advertiser claims and the banana evidence?**

Discuss

Has your school and college got a fast food outlet? What brands are sold? Do you agree these should be available?

Discuss

Do you think the government should be taking a stronger line in regulating television advertising to children? Remember today's obese child will be tomorrow's NHS problem. Or is this like attempting to regulate smoking – too much like 'big brother' trying to control your freedom?

In print the types of pages that appear to be editorial pages but in fact tell you about a particular product are called 'advertorials'.

5.6 What's an advertisement and what's a programme?

One area of advertising that has become more prevalent in the British broadcasting landscape is that of sponsorship of programmes. Sponsorship may well be obvious if it is seen in the credits but not so obvious if it is done through **product placement**.

> What programmes that you currently watch are sponsored and by what product? What do you think are the issues surrounding sponsorship?

In 1996 Heineken was sponsoring a programme called *Hotel Babylon*, which, although made by a British company, was targeted at European youngsters. When an executive of Heineken saw the pilot they were very critical of it. It should, they said, have shown more people drinking lager than wine. That seems rather obvious. But it was the second point that was controversial. They said that there should be fewer 'extraordinary' people and fewer 'Negroes' in the audience. The black musicians were apparently not a problem. As in sport this representation was acceptable. The implication was that black people were on the lower end of the economic scale so that they were not the target market for drinking lager and their presence would put off the white consumers (Blake 1997). Thus, one concern is that the editorial content of the programme was being influenced by the commercial sponsorship.

In January 2004 Cadbury agreed a new sponsorship deal with Granada for a £10 million two year deal to sponsor *Coronation Street*. The deal means that all *Coronation Street* episodes on ITV1 and 2, as well as old ones on Granada Plus, will have the Cadbury '**ident**'. The original sponsorship of £10 million started in 1996 when around 18 million people regularly watched the soap. Today the average figures are around 13 million.

> What was the old sponsorship ident and what is the new ident? Do you think Cadbury's has influenced the editorial content of the programme?

European Television Law as well as the current television codes state that direct sponsorship influence should be avoided. But no large international company will want to see its money support a programme that does not sell or market its product in some form, however tenuous. In the new regulatory system sponsorship that potentially influences the content will be handed over by Ofcom to the ASA (Broadcasting).

The separation of advertisements and programmes is another area for concern. On some channels, such as those devoted to tele-shopping, it is very obvious that all the programmes are advertisements for products or services. In general broadcasting this distinction between advertising and programming could slip if for example the same 'star' who appeared in the programme could also appear in an advertisement or sponsor credits for a product.

At present advertisements must avoid using the conventions of certain programmes, such as those for important news flashes or public service announcements or using people who regularly present these types

NOTES:

of programme. A good example of how an audience can be deceived by the manipulation of generic codes was the infamous *War of the Worlds* radio broadcast on 31 October 1938 in the USA. Orson Welles was the director and he used the convention of news reports interrupting apparent entertainment programmes to tell H.G. Wells' story of the invasion of Earth by Martians. Many listeners who switched on late and so did not hear the initial drama credits really believed they were listening to news flashes and panic ensued.

Gobstopper – Wrigley's ad attracted a record number of complaints. Does this make it a 'success'?

5.7 Statutory and other regulations

In this country we have certain statutory regulations about advertising. There are certain bans such as political advertising and tobacco products and restrictions on the advertising of gambling and lotteries. There is also the Act of Libel and the Trade Descriptions Act. There are quite a number of other regulations, including the self-regulatory system enshrined in the CAP code. To find out more about these codes and the current regulations look on the Ofcom and the ASA websites.

5.8 Can ads shock?

As the ITC was bowing out they listed the top 12 most complained about adverts over its 12 years of existence. Five of these appeared in the year 2003. It seemed that advertisers are increasingly resorting to shock tactics in targeting audience. One of these was a Wrigley advert where a man was seen regurgitating a dog. One that was broadcast just before Christmas 2003 for Mr Kipling cakes, displayed a school nativity play where a woman appeared to be in pain giving birth. This prompted nearly 600 viewer complaints even though the advert had been passed by the Broadcasting Advertising Clearance Centre before it was broadcast. Kipling withdrew the advert.

A toilet tissue advert (Velvet) that showed naked bottoms also attracted complaints. An advert for the magazine *Take a Break* raised complaints when an elderly woman was seen waiting for her meal while the meals-on-wheels driver read her *Take a*

Break. A famous advert which attracted record complaints was the Levi's 'Kevin the Hamster' campaign where a hamster was shown 'dying' of boredom after his wheel broke.

In September 2004 it was reported that Ofcom had banned a television advert for Land Rover featuring a woman firing a gun – 'the glamorisation and normalisation of guns even indirectly is simply offensive to many people' (Ofcom).

Conclusion

'You've been Tangoed'

In this section we have concentrated on the question of regulation of advertising on television. The subject is one that raises many important issues such as media effects, self- or statutory regulation, taste and decency and freedom of expression. Advertising makes up a huge part of the UK economy. In 2002, £16.7 billion was spent on advertising (ASA information). It is becoming an even greater part of the new multi-media world. How can we regulate this world? Does it *need* to be regulated? Should the consumer be protected from false claims or should the consumer be responsible for their own mistakes? Do we have a responsibility to protect the vulnerable and naive? Will changing technologies such as digitalisation and convergence make it impossible to regulate? These are some of the questions that I hope this section has raised for you to discuss. Remember there are no rights or wrongs in this debate.

Activities

Task TV Ads: Scheduling and Young People

- Look at advertisements broadcast around young people's viewing from around 3.30 p.m. to 7.30 p.m.

- How many adverts for fast food such as burgers, crisps, soft drinks, sweets and other convenience foods or chains such as McDonalds are in the advertising breaks?

(a) List the products;
(b) write the slogan/jingle;
(c) analyse the line of appeal for each one.

- Are the lines of appeal in these adverts to taste? Convenience? Cheapness? Celebrity? Glamour? Look at the lists in part 3 targeting audiences for further lines of appeal.

Task Write a Letter - You have the choice:

- Take up the role of *either* a member of the *Anti Fast Food Ads to Kids* campaign *or* the Food Industry's *Pro Food Rights for the Child* group. (Neither of these organisations exist.) Write a letter to Ofcom/ASA Broadcasting expressing your views. Illustrate your points with examples from the adverts that you have analysed.

- *Anti-Fast Food Ads to Kids:*

Do you feel that children are unfairly targeted by these adverts? You were a member of a lobby group for healthier eating what would you say to the regulators and advertisers? Would you want stronger regulation to protect children?

- *Pro-Food Rights for the Child:*

As a producer of a fast food product do you feel children's human rights might be breached by such regulation? Is exercise the answer to obesity and the government should be setting up more sport programmes rather than cutting down on children's pleasures?

Ads that Shock

Task

Look at this list of advertisements that have attracted criticism:

- Kevin the hamster (Levis jeans);

- Velvet toilet tissue;

- Kipling's nativity (cakes);

- Take a Break magazine;

- Wrigley's dog (chewing gum).

Who do you think would complain about each of these adverts?

Appendix 1
A Term's Lesson Outline

This is a suggested route through teaching TV Advertising. As with any lesson plans these are only useful as skeletons on which to hang personal preferences, interests, abilities and specifications. No time limit is given as additional material such as documentaries may take up a substantial amount of one lesson particularly with pausing for discussion and explanation. Preparation beforehand will be required to collect relevant articles, adverts and to photocopy the specific work sheets or discussion points.

The aims are:

- to understand how adverts are constructions using images and sounds to create emotional effects and to persuade purchasing;

- to understand how audiences are constructed and targeted;

- to acknowledge that adverts are value laden;

- to understand how the mass media industry is underpinned by advertising and what are the institutions involved.

Each of the lesson plans is related to a part of the book and the relevant background material, discussion and activity ideas.

Lesson 1 – Introduction to Television Advertising (Introduction and Part 1)

Resources – television adverts pre-recorded.

Aim – to introduce key concepts (see Part 1: Texts, Audiences, Institutions, Ideology.

Objective – to allow students to show how much they already know about this topic and to clarify key terms as they emerge.

Class discussion –

- What is a medium (the means through which messages are delivered – mass media such as…)?

- What is special about television as a medium (audio-visual, new technologies)?

- Why is it important to study television (literacy; democracy; knowledge about others)?

- Are advertisements important in television (where and when do they appear?)?

- Write key questions to ask on board (see end of Part 1).

Show a television advert twice. Ask the key questions for discussion in pairs:

- Who do you think made it and paid for it? Who is it targeted at? What is the purpose? Who will gain from it? Always give reasons why and evidence from the advertisement (e.g. if you think it's targeted at women say what elements tell you this). Feed back answers to the whole class.

Show a different advert twice:

- Individual writing – write a brief discussion about this advert using the key questions and remembering to give evidence.

- Feedback to the class by reading out discussions. Is there agreement as to the answers? If not why not? Does this say anything about the class as an audience?

Homework – choose your own advert to analyse. Record off-air if possible in order to view repeatedly for analysis. To be used for individual analysis and presentation to the class (possible Key Skills Activity).

Lesson 2 – Scheduling and Television as a Medium (Part 1)

Resources – TV listings magazines, scissors and glue.

Aim – to understand how television targets an audience through genres.

Objectives – to ensure students know the difference between PSB and commercial television and satellite and cable channels; and to understand the concept of genre

Class discussion – channels and programmes watched by students. Use the board to list the channels and their identities, e.g. BBC1, Sky, ITV, C5. Ask them who they think is the main audience for each of them. What genres (types) of programme are associated with each? Identify ones with commercials.

Pairs – Do TV Scheduling and Advertising activity, page 14.

Individual – write a justification for their choices.

Homework – do Primary Research activity on page 15 and/or Advertising and Television, page 42.

Lesson 3 – The Other Players – Clients and Agents

Resources – copies of activities listed below.

Aim – to prepare a campaign.

Objective – to allow the students to role play the parts of the main players in producing an advert.

Class discussion – how a campaign is created by an advertising agency and then a proposal given to the client; do Role playing activity, page 14.

Divide into fours – each pair will develop a campaign and present it to the others.

Homework – write up the campaign details and complete the storyboard. The pairs could divide this work between them to present at a later date to the class.

Lesson 4 – Media Language (Part 2)

Resources – a selection of adverts (see Section 2.2 and Resources) and a worked example from a display advertisement; blank storyboards; glossary of camera angles and movements, editing, sound and other technical words appropriate to task. There are many versions of these in media text books showing close-ups, pans, etc.

Aim – to introduce the elements used to construct an advert.

Objectives – to allow students to develop their knowledge of these over several sessions; to build up confidence and skills in analysis

Class discuss the following – introduce the idea of 'text' and 'read'. Use the Glossary words of codes; signs; do TV language activity, page 28.

Hand out the sheets showing the different camera angles.

Hand out or project a worked example of a display advert and go over the elements.

Do a class analysis using a pro forma (see pages 24–27)

In pairs – do Deconstructing Advertisements activity using a photocopied pre-chosen advert.

Homework – find a display advert to analyse individually.

Lesson 5 – Textual Analysis

Resources – A3 plain paper, scissors and glue; a pile of suitable magazine adverts.

Aim – to develop analytical skills.

Objectives – to complete still image analysis and move onto moving television; to use terminology correctly.

Class discussion – check knowledge of camera, colour, framing. Ask for any other elements such as lighting (do activity on page 29 for lighting). Check quality of adverts chosen and substitute if necessary.

Individual – paste adverts onto centre of A3 paper and draw lines to different elements (use the Glossary check list).

Write on the A3 paper what each element means and why it is used (see Deconstructing Advertisements activity, pages 24–27).

Class – watch a television advert. What other elements are present (e.g. moving camera, editing and sound)?

Homework – using the analysis do the extension work (Deconstructing Advertisements activity).

Lesson 6 – Textual Analysis: Sounds

Resources – adverts with a good variety of soundtracks.

Aim – to help students to listen carefully.

Objective – to cut out the images and allow the sounds to tell the story; to extend the vocabulary of sound words.

Class discussion – list as many types of one sound (see The Bells, the Bells, page 30).

In Pairs – write the story using 5 bell sounds activity. Underline each different bell sound. Read out some of the stories to the class.

Class activity – Hearing is Seeing activity, page 30. Give the list to the students for them to fill in depending upon the number of adverts used.

Class discussion – listen to class and accents on the adverts. Discuss how they may be value laden. Do the activity on page 35.

Homework – complete the sound story or choose another sound to use.

Lesson 7 – Editing

Resources – advertisements with different editing styles.

Aim – to understand editing.

Objectives – to show how editing affects interpretation; to show how adverts rely upon juxtaposition to make meanings; to show how ellipses and media literate readers work.

Class – recap on framing and other technical terms.

Define cut, dissolve, fade, jump cut, wipes. Show examples of these transitions and discuss their effects..

Show examples of continuity editing and montage editing.

Show adverts and ask students to identify transitions and styles of editing.

Do Editing activity on page 31.

Homework – sketch an 8 (approx.) frame storyboard for an advert using four different types of transition. Explain why each has been used.

Lesson 8 – Narrative and Genre

Resources – adverts with strong narrative and genre conventions.

Aim – to understand the basic structure of a classic narrative and generic conventions.

Objectives – to analyse narratives in ads and to show how different styles of narrative work, e.g. the problem, the miracle, the joke, the demonstration (see Part 2).

Class discussion – what is a classic narrative? Beginning, middle and end – but not necessarily in that order. Discuss how narratives have basic structures, e.g. the problem or initial equilibrium theories. (there are various charts available for this particularly in film studies books).

Watch adverts with strong narratives and discuss how they work. What are the roles given to the people in the adverts?

In Pairs – develop a narrative for an advert.

Do Narrative activity on page 32.

Class – give out a genre chart check list with typical characters, settings, plots, scenes, dress and object above blank columns. List some genres from class suggestions and ask them to fill in the columns in the chart.

Homework – do Genre activity on page 33 or sketch an advert with generic characteristics.

Lesson 9 – Branding

Resources – bring in objects with brands. Use objects in students' bags which have a brand name.

Aim – to understand branding.

Objectives – to show how important branding is with branding extensions and brand loyalty to the industry; and to identify strong brand names and their characters.

Class discussion – brainstorming brands.

- Discuss brands and how they work. Do Brands activity on page 34

- Do a case study on a well-known brand such as Coca-Cola.

- Brand Appeal activity (page 43) could be done here to introduce students to the next area to be covered – that of audiences.

Homework – students choose a product and research its branding, using the Internet if possible.

Lesson 10 – Audiences and Television (Part 3)

Resources – television adverts targeted at different audiences.

Aim – to understand how audiences are segmented and categorised.

Class – how would you categorise an audience?

Groups – divide into groups and give each group one of the following activities on audiences:

- page 35 activities – psychological; ages and names;

- activity page 46 – lifestyles.

Individual – do Psychographics Campaign activity, page 42.

Homework – complete Psychographics Campaign activity.

Lesson 11 Consolidation

Resources – old television adverts or ones from history of advertising or on postcards, etc.

Aim – to re-cap over adverts and their target audiences; how they are constructed and by whom.

Class activity – Look at old adverts, e.g. from *Washes Whiter*.

Do activity Old vs. New (page 44), either as pairs or individuals.

Appendix 1

Class debate – 'This House believes that Advertising is good for us'.

Lesson 12 – Advertising and Representation (Part 4)

Resources – a range of adverts representing different groups. These could be television or stills.

Aim – to show how adverts deliver and use messages about individuals and groups.

Objectives – to understand glossary words such as stereotype and representation.

Class – discuss this issue using stereotypes familiar to students.

Do Brands and Representation of groups activity on page 56.

Lesson 13 – Advertising and Representation (Part 4)

Resources – a range of old magazines and newspaper to be cut up; large sheets of sugar paper, scissors and glue.

Aim – to show if gender representation exists.

Do Representation of Men activity, page 58. As suggested other groups could also be used and then these could be split between the class to be done simultaneously.

Following this depending upon the class composition specific areas could then be investigated.

Lesson 14 – continuation from 13 (Part 4)

- Representation of Women activities, page 58
- Representation of Families, page 59
- Representation of Men, page 60
- Representation of Race, page 61

Homework – Do the Giving a Talk activity, page 62. (This could be used for Key Skills assessment, but would obviously take some time to cover a whole class presentation.) Schedule produced for presentations.

Lesson 15 – Institutions and the Industry (Part 5)

Resources – television programmes that are currently being sponsored; list of ITC codes for children's advertising see Part 5; ASA schools and colleges might be helpful

(see websites); record adverts broadcast around children's programmes.

Aim – to show the power of advertising and how it is regulated.

Objectives – to ensure students understand the scale of advertising; to arouse interest in how it is regulated; and to introduce a discursive element into the topic.

A) Industry

Class –

- Discuss sponsorship and its role. Show some of the idents on programmes. Discuss consequences of sponsorship.

- Look at some of the statistics on the economic power of advertising (see Part 5). Look at a case study such as Children and Food (see Section 5.5).

B) Regulation – Children and Advertising

Class –

- Show adverts around children's programming. Do the Scheduling activity on page 72.

- Discuss the role of the media in children's lives and link to media effects debates.

Individual/pairs –

- Research the ITC/Ofcom codes on other areas such as alcohol (see websites).

Homework –

- Do the Write a Letter activity on page 72. The class could be divided to get an equal range of opinion and should do their own research on ads on television. (This could also be used as a part of a Key Skills portfolio.)

- Do Ads that Shock activity on page 73.

Lesson 16

Resources – copies of campaigns (see Appendix 2), blank storyboards, crayons. Revision sheets/glossaries or handouts from previous lessons for vocabulary and concepts covered.

Aim – to consolidate and synthesise knowledge into own campaign.

Class – Read over the case studies for the perfume and the blood donor campaign. Revise issues of audience, media language, messages and institutions.

Give out Design a Campaign from Appendix 2, or similar idea. Use the Role Playing activity on page 14.

Individual/Group – use class time to prepare proposals and present ideas or use the format for Shoeshine Corp Rainbow trainers in Appendix 3.

Homework – complete the campaign and write the report.

Hall Advertising Agency 'East Kilbride' shot sequence

• Soundtrack – 'Around the world ...' song

At no time do we see identities of the participants. The focus is always on the case and its travels 'around the world':

• Mid shot from waist down. Man walks l-r and other man walks r-l. Man in centre back picks up brief case (connotes business and travel).

• Holding case across body walks across camera. Fades (connotes fear of security).

• Case goes through security check (connotes air travel).

• Man standing up from cane chair near exotic plants (public place). Picks up case r-l. Woman in Eastern style dress walking away from camera (connotes Eastern country).

• Case with label on baggage loader on runway, plane behind.

• Back of yellow car opened by arm and large stomach wearing red shirt. Case thrown into backseat. Door closed (connotes New York).

• Case falling down rollers top to bottom. More stickers connotes further travel.

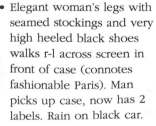

• Elegant woman's legs with seamed stockings and very high heeled black shoes walks r-l across screen in front of case (connotes fashionable Paris). Man picks up case, now has 2 labels. Rain on black car.

• Case upright and turns sideways. Fades.

• Man holding case gets out of London style taxi 'for hire' sign (connotes London).

• Case in hand of man wearing overcoat. Steam. Lifts case up steps into train (connotes old technology; Red Cyrillic script connotes Russia).

• Fades to woman, man in elegant restaurant (connotes wealthy/possible meeting).

Appendix 2

- Man moves to pick up case – no labels (connotes end of travels).

- Man with overcoat over arm goes outside. Sun shining. Fades (connotes optimism).

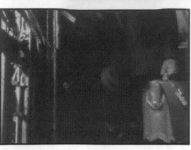

- Case put on tabletop looking out of large picture window. Framed photograph of woman (connotes family and home and rural peace).

- Long shot through window.

Graphics:

'Most top businessmen's briefcases would rather be in East Kilbride.'

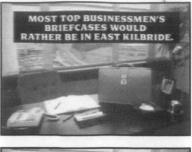

'Scotland's most successful business location.'

The message – after all the travels to exotic cities around the world a businessman will want to come home to the peaceful tranquillity of rural Scotland. The case is the personification or the metonym for business.

NOTES:

Case Study Launching a Campaign

A Perfume Advertisement

Here is an example of an advertising campaign. Read it and then complete your own campaign

Product – Perfume 'X-statique'. This has a strong, heavy scent.

Producer/Client – Gallic of France.

Advertising Agency – Aut and Aut.

Memo

To:	*Aut and Aut Creative Department*
From:	*Account Director*
CC:	
Date:	
Re:	*X-statique*

We have a new client, Gallic of France (owned by a larger corporation). We hope this account will bring us further business from the larger company. Our first job is to provide an advert for their new perfume. As usual the **Account Managers** *will keep a close eye on the budget at all times and any overspend should be referred to them. Please inform the* **Media Buyer** *to buy the relevant slots once work has been started on production, after the approval by the client.*

Campaign Brief
TV campaign for Christmas linked to a display campaign in such vehicles as **The Sunday Times** *magazines and* **Elle** *for October, November and December:*
- *to arouse knowledge about the product in target market;*
- *to provide a strong image;*
- *to target men buying Christmas presents for partners and secondly women buying for selves (these will be Emulators/Achievers; aged 30+; in classes A and B with possibly moving into C1);*
- *to position it as a strong leader in the present market but also able to run on into New Year; to have the ability to diversify into a summer campaign with a change of setting but similar colour combinations.*

Budget
Production Cost – £500,000.
Cost of TV air time – £200,000 with additional repeats built in for four weeks, November to December.
Length of advert – 30 seconds.
Most intense period of repeats to be in late November and early December, the aim being to provide a high profile for Christmas period.

This is a heavily saturated market with strong leaders such as Calvin Klein. The image produced will have to differentiate itself from these and express a line of appeal. Market research has shown there is now a gap in the market following the withdrawal of other perfumes that have become old fashioned in their image. The bottle design is tall and round with a black and gold colour scheme. The name **X-statique** *is printed in red on the black top and there is an imprint of an* **X** *in the glass bottle. Focus group and psychographic research have suggested that warmth, sexuality, class, sophistication, mystery are all ideas implied by this shape and the scent.*

Creative Ideas
The target audiences suggest two ideas: one of availability and one of allure.
The line of appeal will be to class and image. Its personality will be sexy. It will suggest free time and luxury. It will suggest pleasure.

• **Page 1**

Storyboard

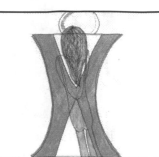

- *Soundtrack: Low saxophone and sultry music with hint of suspense.*
- *Establishing Long Low Shot: Strong reddish sunset over snow scene (suggestion of countryside). Sound effects of footsteps in the snow.*
- *Long shot: Dark hooded figure in long black cloak walks towards chateau style steps (identity could be male/female).*
- *Cut to interior.*
- *Mid shot: Fire crackling (SFX) in grate picking up on black and red colours from first scene. Pan to –*
- *Close-up: Hand with cloak (out of focus) moves towards the perfume bottle in focus in foreground (again could be male/female). Cut to –*
- *Long shot: Back view of woman dressed in tight fitting red trouser one piece with black hair seen through the bottle so that her shape fits the bottle. The firelight flickering off the bottle suggesting the warm and heavy scent of the perfume.*
- *Still of woman in same outfit lying on the letter **X** of the word **X-statique** and 'by Gallic of France' beside the image. Graphics are of handwriting script. This reflects the magazine campaign.*
- *Female Voice Over: French accent, low dark tones – 'Whoever you are, it is **X-statique**'.*

Presentation to the Client – *The Way this Campaign will Work:*
- *The appeal to luxury and status through the setting.*
- *The emotional appeal of snow and firelight for winter/Christmas.*
- *We have the enigma that the hooded character could be a man or a woman to hook the audience into further adverts.*
- *The promise that the product will induce ecstasy (**X-statique**) either for the man who will be buying the illusion of the woman in the bottle or for the woman who will be buying the promise of allure with the perfume.*
- *The colours will reflect that of the product, i.e. black/red/gold.*
- *The setting and colours will suggest the scent's characteristics, i.e. heavy and warm.*
- *Use of intertextuality – **The French Lieutenant's Women** and other film images of hooded characters and also link to France.*
- *The red costume (connotes sexuality and availability).*
- *The **X** will be a strong logo/product image to be maintained in future campaigns. (Possibility of dropping the **statique** although this spelling does connote French.)*
- *The French connections and the 'heritage' and cultural factors of France and perfume, and French and romance emphasised with the accent.*

Why Television?
'Television advertising directly affects the way we shop. A recent study showed that television produced on average a 4.8% uplift in sales in the first 4 weeks after advertising is seen and a significant number of incremental purchases for some time after.' (source: Anglia TV website)

• Page 2

Have a Go! Launching a Campaign.

Here is your brief:

Memo

To: _All Departments_
From: _Accounts Director_
CC:
Date:
Re: _Rainbow_

We have a new shoe manufacturer client, **Shoeshine Corp**_. They are launching a new trainer for the fashion market called_ **Rainbow**_:_

- _it has waterproof qualities;_
- _it can be bought in different shades;_
- _it has male and female styles;_
- _it is produced under strict Fair Trade regulations._

Shoeshine Corporation _would like a brief in the next week. Their budget is £50,000:_

- _Choose and design a logo._
- _Decide on the target market._
- _Decide on the line of appeal._
- _Decide on a slogan._
- _Work out a storyboard to deliver the image – remember technical codes of camera, lighting, mise-en-scène, soundtrack, etc._
- _Consider using celebrities, narratives, genres, intertextuality._
- _Decide upon costings (e.g. if you have a star you will have less money for location shooting)._
- _The television ratings will vary depending upon the times you think the target market will be watching. You can investigate these on the web, e.g. Carlton or Sky web sites._
- _Draw a detailed storyboard and script. Do not forget to mention voices, etc._
- _Write a report to the client explaining your justifications and thinking behind the campaign. Record all your decisions._
- _Present the storyboard and report to your client._

• **Page 1**

Appendix 4

Tetley

Mascot Campaign advertisement 1999

This was part of the sponsorship of Rugby by Tetleys. At the time Tetleys was the official beer and sponsor of rugby union cup competitions. The campaign also included a photo of Martin Johnston, then Captain of the English Team, lying down naked except for a strategically placed bottle of Tetleys. It was part of the 'blood, sweat and beers' campaign and one where the slogan 'Tetley Beer – Smoothly Does It' was used in several adverts.

Shot sequence:

- LS following large mascot bear cutting through cheering crowd wearing English St George's flags. Camera pulls back. (Figure 1)

- Twickenham sign shown shows it's a rugby crowd and an international event. Camera moves forward.

- Montage of shots including high angle shot of bear approaching gatekeeper. Authorised personnel sign seen. (Figure 2)

- POV shot through bear's mouth approaching gate – identifies there is a person inside costume with whom we (the audience) identify. (Figure 3)

- See bear's face in CU to establish the POV. (Figure 4)

- Bear approaches gatekeeper in yellow jacket followed by two men waving tickets.

- POV shot of gatekeeper from inside the bear costume. (Figure 5)

- Gatekeeper allows bear in.

- Back view as bear pushes through crowd to bar counter. (Figure 6)

- Reverse shot of two men on either side pushed away by bear – who holds up three fingers to camera. These are Bill Beaumont ex-Captain of England on the right and Micky Skinner ex-English International on the left. (Figure 7)

- Men look surprised (CU of one man) and pleased – three fingers means a beer for each of them (including the bear).

- Blonde bar maid smiles at camera and puts three Tetley beers on the bar counter. (Figure 8)

- Bear takes off head to reveal three men inside costume.

- CU of three heads - joke is the three beers are all for the bear. (Figure 9)

- Shot of three men in costume and two men on either side. Holding up beer as if saying cheers to viewer.

- Slogan – Tetley beer smoothly does it. (Figure 10)

Figure 1

Figure 6

Figure 2

Figure 7

Figure 3

Figure 8

Figure 4

Figure 9

Figure 5

Figure 10

The combination of patriotism, male camaraderie and comedy is the appeal of 'Tetley Beer – Smoothly Does It' advert.

The joke is that three men get into the bar at Twickenham disguised as a mascot. They did it 'smoothly' just as the beer is 'smooth'. This was part of a running Tetley campaign where doing something 'smoothly' was used. The word 'smooth' has colloquial connotations of being clever, and able to pull off something a little bit cheeky, e.g. 'that was a bit of smooth driving'. It is also used to suggest a quality of the beer as being easy to drink and not rough to taste. So there is a pun involved. The target audience are male drinkers and sports fans. This is because of the central characters and the knowledge of the game required to fully understand the advert. But other groups would get the main joke.

The camera style is juxtaposition of opposite angles, movements, framing and positions that are montaged by editing to create a dynamic feel and to cover the ellipses in the narrative. The narrative is: how do three fans get into Twickenham without tickets? Who is the bear? Their cheeky action and Tetley beer are endorsed by the celebrities at the bar. The audience need to know about Twickenham and rugby; the symbolic significance of the flag; and that animal mascots of people in costumes parade around games and act as cheerleaders. The music is jolly and creates a rhythm against which to tell the narrative. Beliefs about patriotism are suggested, rugby as a national sport, also ideas of who plays rugby and who are the supporters.

There are significantly no black or minority groups represented. The only significant female is blonde, young and physically attractive and serving the men. The heroes are 'lads'.

Glossary

agency	The company that organises the advertising campaign for a **client**.
anchorage	Words which fix the meaning of an image rather than leave it 'free floating'.
animatic	The filmed storyboard with stills or a rough cut to show the customer for approval before full filming.
appreciation index (AI)	How much the audience likes a television show.
audience	The group that the advertisement and campaign is targeted at.
binary opposition	Two opposing elements which work because of the knowledge of the other. Used by Lévi-Strauss in the study of societies.
brand/brand image	The name and image of a product with a distinct identity from competitors and with a personality and emotion attached. Also: brand positioning, where it is in the market; brand loyalty, customers buy on a regular basis e.g. soap powder; brand awareness in the customer to identify its particular characteristics; brand leader, such as McDonalds in fast food; brand extension/stretching such as Coke into Diet Coke.
brief	The outline of the campaign given to the agency by the client with its aim.
bricolage	Putting together and using objects or images (do-it-yourself).
campaign	A run of ads over a specified time.
client	The company or organisation such as a charity that pays for the campaign.
codes encoding/ decoding	The elements that make up an advert and the creating and reading of these. They can include technical and generic elements.
commercial/ commercial break	Another word for an advertisement.
conglomerate	A large organisation made up of several smaller organisations.
connotation	The meaning suggested by an element in the text (see **denotation**).
conventions	The use of elements which by repetition become expected.
convergence	The joining together of media into one route to the consumer.
copy	The words written for the advert by the copy-writer.
consumer	The user of the products.
cultural imperialism	The idea of cultural messages being given by a dominant group to others with the danger of the minority identity being swamped.
decoding	Taking apart and reading the different elements of a text.
demographics	The way an audience is divided up or described by gender, age, race, location, etc.
denotation	The elements seen in the advert (see **connotation**).
discourse	The messages that accumulate around an idea from different sources which create a belief, often a false belief such as a stereotype.
effects	See **media effects**.
ellipsis/es	Gap(s) which the reader of an advert fills in mentally to make sense.
encoding	Putting the elements together for meaning into a text.

focus group	Small, selected target groups for market research.
fctishism	Objects become more important than the real. For example, blonde hair on women or muscles on men.
genre	The type of story being told, or the type of text.
globalisation	World control of products, companies and/or communications by one dominant group.
hegemony (Antonio Gramsci)	The way that ideas (ideologies) can be transmitted in society through influential groups such as the media and journalists.
icon/iconic	Image which stands for an idea.
ident	Identity of a brand.
ideology	Belief created by repetition of ideas (see **discourse** and **stereotype**).
intertextuality	The link between texts which help to move meanings between texts.
jingle	The musical or rhythmic words using a catchphrase.
juxtaposition	Elements purposefully put next door to each other to create a new meaning.
key lighting	The most important light in the frame. Can be strong (high key) or weak (low key).
linearity	Following a time line or similar structure.
logo	The symbol used to identify a brand, such as the Nike 'tick'.
market research	The work done by sociologists, psychiatrists and others to find out about the target audience.
mass	Large, broad audience group.
media effects	This area is a major study in itself and we shall only briefly touch upon it. The *hypodermic model* believes that viewers (especially children) will see something and be directly influenced by the media. It suggests that audiences are therefore passive viewers. The *uses and gratification theory* suggests a more active role for the viewer, as the consumer uses the media to gratify their own personal needs. The *inoculation theory* suggests a long term effect of media. These models suggest immediate copycat behaviour or more long term de-sensitisation effects and culturalisation.
metonym	An image standing for an idea/concept. For example a crown stands for royalty and patriotism.
mise-en-scène	Those elements put into the frame for their particular meaning such as composition or colour or objects.
niche	Small, narrow audience group.
non verbal communication (NVC)	Dress, hair, eyes, actions of a person in the advert.
off-peak	Periods of lower audience numbers watching television and therefore cheaper time slots for adverts.
peak/prime time	Television mass audiences and therefore expensive advertising slots.
polysemic	Something which can have many meanings or readings.
product placement	Placing a product in a programme so that it can be deliberately seen by the audience, such as a bottle of whisky in a pub with its label to the camera.
psychographics	The study of how a target audience shares certain values or likes.

Glossary

qualitative research	Looking at small areas of study such as focus groups.
quantitative research	Research over large numbers of the target audience such as with questionnaires.
rate card	Produced by television broadcasters to show how much each of the time slots cost and to show how they can package time slots together.
realism	Using elements to suggest that what is seen reflects the real world through technical codes or other devices.
representation	How groups or institutions are created through the media.
schedule	Time management in television programming. *Hammocking* is where a certain programme is put between two perhaps stronger others; *pre-echo* encourages early viewing so as not to miss a later programme; *inheritance* is where audiences will stay with a station, perhaps after viewing a soap; *common junction points*, where programmes on different stations change at the same time.
semiotics/semiology (Ferdinand de Saussure)	The study of signs through a 'scientific' approach.
sign	Each element is a sign which tells us about the product.
slice of life	Sometimes used by advertisers to portray 'real' people as opposed to actors talking about the product.
slogan	The copy line which summarises the campaign.
slomo	Slow motion.
sponsorship	The method of a company giving money for an event or a programme in return for their name to be associated with that programme, e.g. Beamish with *Inspector Morse*.
stereotype	A simplified and fixed representation.
symbol	Standing for something, such as a flag for patriotism.
synergy	The joining together of several groups (conglomerates) creates a power over markets beyond each individual company as they feed to and on each others profits.
text	The advert as a whole which is 'read' by the audience.
voice-over	The speaker is never seen. We only hear his (usually his) disembodied voice.
voyeur	The way that the viewer has power to look at the image to gain pleasure.
watershed	The agreed time (self-regulation) after which adult content programmes can be shown. On terrestrial television this is 9 p.m. Sky has chosen to use 8 p.m.

Bibliography and References

Adorno, T. *The Culture Industry: Selected essays on Mass Culture*, London, Routledge 1991.

Barthes, R. *Mythologies*, London: Cape, 1972.

Berger, J. *Ways of Seeing*, London: Penguin, 1972.

Blake, A. 'Listen to Britain' in Niva, M.; Blake, A. MacRury, I; Richards, B. (eds) *Buy this Book: Studies in Advertising and Consumption*, London: Routledge, 1997.

Brierley, S. *The Advertising Handbook*, London: Routledge, 1995.

Branston, G. and Stafford, R. *The Media Students Book*, London: Routledge, 1996

Buckingham, D. and Bragg, S. *Young People, Media and Personal Relationships*, commissioned by the BSC; ITC; BBFC;BBC and ASA, Institute of Education, London University, 2003.

Carter, H. 'Eat now, play later' in *The Guardian*, 30 April 2003.

Cozens, C. 'Ofcom proposes wider role for ASA' in *The Guardian* 27 October 2003.

Cohen, S. *Folk Devils and Moral Panics: The Creation of the Mods and Rockers*, London: Routledge, 1972

Davis and Walton, *Language, Image and Media*, London: Blackwell, 1983.

Dominick and Rauch, 'The Image of Women in Network TV Commercials', *Journal of Broadcasting*, 16, 259-265.

Douglas, T. *The Complete Guide to Advertising*, London: Macmillan, 1984.

Dyer, G. *Advertising as Communication*, London: Methuen, 1982.

Dyer, R. *The Matter of Images: Images on Representation*, London: Routledge, 1992.

Fiske, J. *Introduction to Communication*, London: Methuen, 1982.

Grahame, J. *Advertising*, London: English and Media Centre, 1993.

Griffiths, M. Kolbe, Richard H. and Darrell Meuhling 'Gender Roles and Children's Television Advertising'. *Journal of Current Issues and Research in Advertising*, 17(1), 50-59 (1995).

Hindle, S. 'Snap! Ad agencies caught using copycat photographs' in *The Sunday Times*, 6 November 1994.

Hoek , J. and Lawrence, K. *Television Advertising to Children: An Analysis of Selected New Zealand Commercials*, website www.marketing-bulletin.massey.ac.nz,1998.

Holme, B. *Advertising Reflections of a Century*, London: Viking, 1982.

Kellner, D. *Media Culture*, London: Routledge, 1995.

Mattelart, A. *Advertising International The Privatisation of Public Space* (tr. Michael Chanan), London: Routledge, 1991.

Mulvey, L. 'Visual Pleasures in Narrative Cinema' *Screen*, Vol16 No. 3 1975.

Myers, G. *Ad Worlds*, London: Arnold, 1999.

Nava, M. Blake, A; MacRury I; Richards, B. (eds) *Buy This Book: Studies in Advertising and Consumption*, London: Routledge, 1997.

Nevett T.R. *Advertising in Britain: A History*, London: Heinneman, 1982.

O'Donohoe, S. 'Leaky Boundaries: Intertextuality and young adult experiences of advertising' in Nava, M; Blake, A; ManRury, I; Richards, B. (eds) *Buy The Book: Studies in Advertising and Consumption*, London: Routledge, 1997.

Ogilvy, D. *Confessions of an Advertising Man*, London: Longman, 1963.

Packard, V. *The Hidden Persuaders*, London: Longman, 1957.

Quart, A. *Branded: The Buying and Selling of Teenagers*, London: Arrow, 2003.

Sibley, B. *The Book of Guinness Advertising*, London: Guinness Superlatives, 1985.

Trowler, *Investigating the Media*, London: Unwin Hyman, 1988.

Williamson, J. *Decoding Advertisements Ideology and Meaning in Advertising*, London: Marion Boyars, 1978.

Young, B. *Television Advertising and Children*, Oxford: OUP (Clarendon Press), 1991.

Bibliography and References

RESOURCES

The Video Studio – Contact details
The Video Studio
Richmond-upon-Thames College
Egerton Road
Twickenham, Middx. TW2 7SJ
Tel 020 8607 8423 Fax: 8422
e-mail video@rutc

It is necessary to pay for registrations but then one can buy old off air recordings such as the *Washes Whiter* series and more specific campaigns such as Benetton. Some other general advertising programmes which cover areas discussed in this book and that are available include:

- Charities – 'Poor Dear' (1994)

- Stereotypes – 'Playing the Part' (1994)

- Advertising to 18-29s – 'Generation X' (1995)

- Use of Language in Advertising – 'Whose English' part 6 (1997)

- Children's adverts – 'Pester Power' (1998) and 'Getting Older Younger' (1999)

- Sex images in ads – 'Sex Sells' (2001)

- General Election 2001 – 'Tony in Adland' (2002)

- History of adverts – 'Ads that changed the world' (2003)

- Controls on adverts – 'Ads they had to Ban' (2003)

It is also possible to collect a reel of ads tailor made through such companies as **Digireel** (020 7437 7743) www.dig.co.uk, and **Xtreme.com** (020 7871 8080). There is a cost to this service of approximately £20 per advert.

Grahame, J. *Advertising Pack*, The English and Media Centre, London, 1993. This has a range of classroom activities focusing mainly on display adverts.

Balzagette, Cary (ed.) *Media Education: An Introduction*, The Open University/BFI, 1992. There is an Italian pasta advert on video tape and a detailed analysis of this advert in the text.

Campaign - the weekly magazine of advertising.

Boyd-Barrett, O. *Communication and Education* EH207 O.U. 1987 Television Programme 6 and study guide and Block 6 — Tetley Tea Bags campaign and audio cassette 3 band 10 'Tea-folk talk'. This is an excellent case study on how a campaign is put together. Although now out of print it may be available through local libraries.

The Media File published by Mary Glasgow Publications Ltd (1989 and 1991) and Stanley Thomas (Publishers) Ltd. (1993). A series of photocopiable classroom activities with sections on advertising which are still relevant if available.

Race in the Frame BBC publication with videos and workbooks. As a non-commercial organisation this does not cover adverts but does cover the issue of representation of race in television comprehensively.

Advertising Standards Authority – This was established in 1961. A semi-independent watchdog set up by the Advertising Association. In charge of print adverts (to date) there is an excellent resource area on its website for educational use. www.asa.org.uk

WEBSITES:

This is not a comprehensive list. Many of the sites are referenced in the body of the book. There are also additional sites that may prove useful for resources and research. Some sites require subscription whilst other sites are obviously there to promulgate specific viewpoints. As always, ask questions of the source as well as the content of any website. Search engines such as Yahoo! and Google and www.alltheweb.com are all useful starting points.

www.benetton.co.uk – the company with controversial adverts in the past.

www.rutc.ac.uk – Richmond on Thames College which runs the Video Studio, a huge resource for old television programmes.

www.buble.ac.uk – university academic site.

www.knowuk.co.uk – subscription site.

http://pcift.chadwyck.co.uk – subscription site.

www.sosig.ac.uk – social sciences site.

www.asa.org.uk – The Advertising Standards Authority – go for the Schools and Colleges site for information and worksheets on print advertising; also case studies.

www.cap.org.uk – the code for advertisers.

www.ofcom.org.uk – new regulatory authority for broadcasting.

www.barb.co.uk – audience research site.

www.guardianunlimited.co.uk – site for news, research with links.

www.bbc.co.uk – useful links and information on media.

www.ipa.co.uk – Institute of Practitioners in Advertising.

www.warc.com — organisation for advertisers.

www.popcultures.com – type in 'advertising' to get a list of articles and links.

www.media.guardian.co/advertising – full of excellent articles and links.

www.mudvalley.co.uk – excellent research site for students.

www.mediaknowall.com – excellent site for Media Studies students with links, glossaries, case studies - linked to the Welsh Board syllabus.

www.uta.edu.english/dab/illuminations/kell6 – critical theory of advertising

www.mediawatch-uk.org – campaign organisation to safeguard content of the media.

www.memory.loc.gov – American site with information such as 50 years of Coca-Cola ads.

www.hp.com – Hewlett Packard site with adverts go to newsroom and then to ads. Other products will have similar sites.

www.newint.org – *New Internationalist* a magazine with an alternative agenda to look at global issues.

www.fairtrade.org.uk – Fair Trade the organisation aimed at helping producers in the Third World get a reasonable price for their products.

www.dci-au.org – Television Without Frontiers TV advertising and the protection of children in the European Union.

www.btaa.co.uk – British television advertising awards.

www.advertisingarchives.co.uk –the advertising archives.

www.hatads.org.uk – the history of advertising.